When Grandma Teaches You to Lie
or not really

JENNY PREVATTE

SPARK Publications
Charlotte, North Carolina

When Grandma Teaches You to Lie
Jenny Prevatte

Copyright © 2018 by Jenny Prevatte. All rights reserved. No part of this book may be used or reproduced in any manner whatsoever without written permission from the author, except in the case of brief quotations embodied in critical articles or reviews. For permissions requests, please contact the author at jenny@twilitecs.com.

Designed, produced, and published by SPARK Publications
Illustrations by James Denk
SPARKpublications.com
Charlotte, NC

Some names have been changed to protect the privacy of individuals and their families.

Printed in the United States of America.
Paperback, June 2018, ISBN: 978-1-943070-44-2

Biography & Autobiography / Personal Memoirs
Biography & Autobiography / Women
Family & Relationships / Parenting / Grandparenting

DEDICATION

Obviously, I'm dedicating this to Grandma!
She was perfect—smart, funny, loving. She allowed me
to be the "independent" little person I was and to grow into
the independent adult person I am.

I loved her so much. And I miss her still.

Table of Contents

Dedication 2
Chickens Like It Hot 7
Shooting the Breeze 17
Making Biscuits 23
The Message in the Book 29
Christmas Note from Grandma. 32
Diamond Rings and Salesmen 35
Dogs in the Garden 41
It's OK 47
Miss Gladys 51
Christmas Note from Grandma. 55
Grandma Lied to Her Best Friend 57
Tobacco Worms 61
Good Pop on the Rear End. 69
Saving a Missing Tooth 75

Christmas Note from Grandma	79
Interrogation!	81
Free Snob	85
After-Christmas Sales	91
Meanness	97
Christmas Note from Grandma	101
Cancer	103
You Will Have Children	107
Hiding Behind the Staircase	111
My Fav! Sweet Tater Pies!	119
Christmas Note from Grandma	127
Kitty	129
You Don't Need My Phone Number	133
Masking Tape	139
Christmas Note from Grandma	142
Adult Female	145
I Wonder	157
About the Author	158

Chickens Like It Hot

Grandma was the coolest woman I've ever known. To this day, I still hear some of the things she would say and can apply them to almost any situation I'm in. Her lessons have shown me "the way" many times. And I have so many things from her I apply to personal and business life.

The fun part—for me at least—is the sarcasm. She was one of the most sarcastic people I've ever known. You'll see that as we go. Some of the lessons I learned and still apply were *very* sarcastic. I think you'll enjoy her point of view on some things.

Personal disclaimer here: Grandma was not politically correct and not always tactful, nor did she care if you agreed with anything she thought or did. I inherited all of that and more! I don't intentionally try to insult anyone or step on anyone's feelings. But sometimes I do. I also don't claim any rights to tell you right or wrong with your own opinions, habits, or likes. I don't care if you agree with me. I don't care if you have the same opinions. I don't care if you like ketchup (I don't). Does that make sense?

I think we can still cohabitate just fine on this planet with our differences. I will not apologize for my opinions or my likes and dislikes, nor will I apologize for my attitude. They are mine, and I claim them.

So here is my suggestion: if anything in the following pages offends your fine and delicate sensibilities, quit reading, close the book, and move on with your day. Yes, it is sarcasm. But it's simple, and it works.

Now that we have that handled, let me set up Grandma's world for you. Grandma was a farmer's wife, a normal, North Carolina, Southern farm wife—no frills, no fluff, not a lot of "grey" area.

Granddaddy passed when I was little—cancer of some kind. I don't have any actual memories of him, just impressions from photos and stories.

By the time I was born, the farm focused on chickens and tobacco as cash crops and a few cows, pigs, and hens for meat and dairy. Tobacco fields surrounded the house and all the buildings. There was one field between Grandma's house and Ms. B's house. I'll introduce Ms. B later. That was the only field I was allowed in alone, to go to Ms. B's. The doors and porches to the two houses were in eyeshot of each other. And I could hear Grandma if she called me. That was the important part!

There were also several acres of gardens scattered around on the property. Some of them down in hollows (or little valleys for you non-farmers). Others were part of a field or just stuck between buildings. There was usually something growing nine to ten months of the year.

There were three chicken houses on the property. I think—I'm not certain—they housed 10,000 chickens each. That's a drop in the bucket compared to houses today, but at the time, that was a lot of chickens! I remember the houses were HOT and muggy. Apparently chickens like hot temperatures. I was only allowed to go in with Grandma. She had to go in at least twice a day and check on them, make sure the feed and water were OK, and gather and remove any sick or dead animals. When you came out, you spent at least five minutes cleaning the bottom of your shoes, in my case cleaning bare feet. Grandma made me go in barefooted. She said bare feet were easier to clean. Nasty stuff—think about it! But such was her world.

She lived in a house with some layout oddities. I think they built the house themselves. And I know Granddaddy built onto it later. It was a big figure six. The very front room (a formal living room type of room) wasn't used by the time I was born. At all. It was dark and dusty and closed off most of the time. What had been my mother's bedroom was on the far side of the front room—the top of the six.

The living room was added on later—a big, bright room spanning almost the whole length of that end of the house. Three doors in the room led to Grandma's bedroom, outside, and to the kitchen. There was also an outside window on the inside wall—I'll go there shortly. This room is where the phone lived. I'll go there later. You'll enjoy both of those stories.

Leaving the living room on the left side, you went into the kitchen. From the kitchen, there was a door to the back porch and then to outside. That back door was the one used most often and had cinderblock steps. We sat on those steps *a lot*. She liked to sit there and just enjoy the day.

I always found it funny that Grandma's refrigerator lived on the back porch. The porch was closed in and secured with a door that locked, but it was something I thought was odd. The back porch was also where the clothes-washing machine was. The dryer was outside strung between trees or poles or buildings—low tech but effective.

Through the kitchen the other way was the den and a short hallway around to Grandma's bedroom, a bedroom that had been my uncle's, and the bathroom. And through Grandma's bedroom, you got back into the living room on the other side (now you see the loop in the six). The other side of the den went into the closed-off front room.

The hallway was a focal point and the single source of heat for the house. A wood stove sat there. She had a furnace in the basement and heater vents along the baseboards in most rooms. But she didn't use it. In the winter, most rooms were closed off except the den, kitchen, her bedroom, and the bathroom. Across from the stove was a steep stairway to the attic. Hated the attic. Dark, musty smelling. And *that* is where the silver tinsel Christmas tree lived. Whew—horrid tree. We'll go there later too.

Another oddity compared to the houses you've probably lived in: Grandma did not have hot water. She heated water if you needed hot water. And just for the record, washing your long hair in cold water in the winter is not fun!

And speaking of washing your hair, let's all go to the bathroom. Remember the outside window on the inside wall in the living room?

That was the window in the bathroom! Apparently, that had been an outside wall, and Granddaddy just kept the window right where it was. A couch sat on that wall in the living room under that window. It was so embarrassing if you needed to use the bathroom while anyone was in the living room. It had the glass panes, was shut, and had shutters. But still! Just the thought of sharing those sounds with anyone visiting was beyond embarrassing. I still giggle every time I think of that window.

She also didn't have air conditioning, at all. Grandma's standard responses: open a window or go outside. And honestly, outside was wonderful in the summer. She had shade elms all around the house, a swing on the front porch and in the backyard, and folding yard chairs everywhere. There was no reason to be cooped up inside! And on a farm, you did not have time to hang out in the house anyway.

Grandma loved flowers and flowering plants. There were all kinds of pretty blooming things in her yard. And after a few years, she had dozens of hummingbirds each summer. She hung feeders all in the trees and around those flowering plants. They were fun to watch until the little suckers started dive-bombing you. If the feeders were empty, it got dangerous.

I was told Granddaddy loved trees. Along with the shade elms he loved, he had pecan and walnut trees all over the place. There were a couple of apple trees around the tobacco barns. There was a garden behind the barn and pigpen. Cutting through the middle was a patch with several pecan trees. Every year, we'd go out and pick up all the pecans. When I was little, I was sent up the tree to shake the limbs for any ripe enough to fall off. That is big fun for a little person, shaking nuts down onto the adults' heads.

Coming out of the house, to the left were the garage, woodpile, pump house, and storage building. The garage was an open shed type of building. There was a room in the back my mother and uncle used as a playhouse when they were little. The storage building (or smoke house) was for storing the canned goods, canning supplies, and hung meat. There were usually several ham shoulders hanging in there.

Down the dirt road a few feet was another open garage and storage building. Grandma's laying hens had a coop in the back of that building. They had the normal inside shelving and nesting with a fenced in area to let them go outside. I wasn't allowed in there much. She also had some chickens roaming the yard most summer months.

An aside here: I was also told Granddaddy liked guineas. Stupid birds! They would sit in the road and watch as a car ran over them. We had to shoo them out of the way just to park in the driveway. But apparently, he thought they were good watch dogs. They made a horrible racket if you got them stirred up. For several years, we had guineas roaming the yard. As they died off, Grandma just didn't replenish the numbers. They were finally gone.

Farther down was the barn, a pigpen area, a tractor shed, a tobacco barn, and two chicken houses. All along the sides of the road were fields—tobacco, corn, garden, peas, or whatever was in season. It was a nice place to be. I would not want to be a farmer today, but growing up on that farm was perfect! Life seemed slower and easier, not much "noise" to mess with.

So that's a snapshot of Grandma's world—and as often as possible, my world. What follows are stories of time spent with Grandma on her farm. Some of them are just things she did or said that I think are funny or insightful. Others are stories that taught some valuable lessons—most I still carry with me today. Those of you who know me will see how and why I do and say certain things. You'll finally understand me! Not sure if that's good or bad, but there it is.

I loved her so much. And I miss her still. I hope you'll enjoy these stories around a lot of my life lessons.

MEMORY MOMENTS

Winters at Grandma's were rough if you had long hair like I did. She didn't have hot water. I had to wash my hair in the kitchen sink. Then all that long hair would hang down my back—wet and cold. I'd spend the next hour or so sitting beside the wood stove waiting on my hair to dry. Maybe that's why she kept hers up in curlers so much.

Shooting the Breeze

Let me set up the town Grandma lived in. It was small. One stoplight. Another blinking caution light where the main road split off into a Y formation. NO fast-food franchise or chain places.

They had one "burger joint." Grandma loved it! When I was in college, I'd come down and take her to eat there. She thought it was wonderful. Personally, I think the memories of it are the best part. It is still there and looks to be booming when I drive by. There are still no other fast-food type places there.

The grocery store was an independent. It was good enough. You'll learn later on, she didn't buy much at the grocery store anyway. And she didn't eat much junk, like tater chips and things, so those entire aisles weren't even on her radar when she went in. Her things were the staples.

There was a "farm supply and feed" store. I think every small town has a store like this. You can get almost anything there. If you've never been to one, it's a fun combination of stores: feed for livestock, seeds for gardens, hardware, household stuff, farm supply, and anything else you could imagine. They even had a candy counter! I *loved* going in that store! There were all kinds of interesting things to look at. That was also the only store where I was allowed to wander around by myself. To this day I love to plunder in those old stores. It's fascinating what you find.

Grandma was one of the locals. She always parked at and came in the back door, at the loading dock. But remember, back then, you didn't have the same issues with theft and mischief a lot of places have now. Customers came and went as they pleased. She usually went in for garden supplies and seeds or plants. That's where I learned the name of my favorite field peas—Dixie Leas!

There were *two* gas stations. That was serious. She had her favorite—we'd go in and get a soft drink and nabs or something when she needed gas. Everyone knew each other. She would stop and "visit" with the person working that day while someone put gas in her car.

Note here: Granddaddy liked the other station a little better. I think because it was usually filled with men (his buddies) sitting around "shooting the breeze."

I have to share here—the pea green house. With any small town there are short cuts to get anywhere. Almost any time Grandma and I would go anywhere if we could take a particular shortcut, we would. I loved—I have no idea why—to go past this ugly, faded pea-green house. I have no idea who lived in it. Grandma probably did. But she'd slow down: "Jenny, there's that ugly little house." Then we'd talk junk about it the rest of the trip. No lessons there—just playful fun.

As with any other town, small or otherwise, there were all the normal places—post office, drug store (only one), bank (only one), and a doctor's office (only one). The places I listed above are the places we went to the most. And there were other normal things such as schools and churches.

One of the funniest things I remember about Grandma's "small town" is you physically went to pay your monthly bills. She would go to the power company and pay her bill, or to the phone company—at least the ones that had city counters in town. And the person at the counter would chitchat, and they'd "visit" for a few minutes—great way to catch up on gossip!

Lesson point to bring this all back around to my world now: I was listening to an employee at a local electric co-op close to where I live now. He was trying to describe the clientele they have to someone who was visiting. He said they have three different client types. The first one is older; they still come in to pay their bill at the counter and still expect the person to know their name and maybe even ask about something personal like how their grandson is doing in baseball camp.

The second type will pay their bill by mailing a check; they don't need or want a lot of personal contact. But when they do need something, they expect that same level of personal "care" as the first group—know their name, listen to their issue, and help solve the problem. That's the group I'm in.

The third type is younger and wants everything online. They'll pay online and submit issues online. They don't want and don't care to have a personal relationship with the company.

I remember thinking—that's the perfect explanation of that small town Grandma lived in! When I visit now, that's exactly what I see. But I also have that in my own world. I have client sets just like that. Some want me to be very personal and others just want the service I provide. I think we need all three types. It adds variety and brings us—or at least me—back to basics.

It was a nice little town. Still is as far as I can tell. They have two stoplights now! But that same little burger joint is still the only one in town. And the grocery store is still an independent and the only one in town. While I'm usually all over change, sometimes non-change is good too.

Making Biscuits

Ms. B and Mr. F were, by the time I knew them, an older, black couple who lived on Grandma's farm. I think they lived there for many years. Their children grew up with my mother and my uncle. So they were probably about Grandma's age. I must apologize—I do not know their full names or even their last name. I was little the last time I saw them and just never learned more. But they were very special to me! I think now, knowing their names might not matter. It's the memories of them that matter most.

Loved Ms. B! She always wore a dress or skirt and usually had several layers of aprons. She never wore pants! And she usually had peppermints or hard candy in one or more pockets all wrapped up in tissue. And snuff in another. That gold snuff can was always with her. And she usually had a "snuff bump" in her lower lip. She also kept a scarf or kerchief on her head all the time.

I was allowed—from very early on—to cross the tobacco field between her house and Grandma's and go visit. When I did, and when she was making biscuits, which seemed like all the time, she would make one especially for me. Yep, just for me! They were so good. Warm, fluffy—good stuff! I have a vague memory of me carrying them around eating on them while I played. In my memory, they were *huge* biscuits. They were probably the normal size, just huge to a little person.

She cooked on a wood stove in a kitchen that looked like it was actually an enclosed porch. The water was outside and came from a hand pump. The house had no plumbing.

And if it wasn't biscuits, she was always messing with plants. She had hanging and potted plants all over the place. You've probably seen them—swedish ivy and wandering jew (the one with purple leaves). The others I remember so well were succulents called "hen and biddies." Every year she would fix me a few clippings to take and replant. I had some of those plants through college.

Ms. B was my partner in crime on a couple of occasions. She took me out on her rowboat fishing at least once. There were a couple little ponds on the farm. This was, of course, after being told by Grandma not to take me. Apparently, I wanted to go, and she took me. I couldn't swim yet. I didn't learn to swim until first or second grade. I lived—didn't fall in or anything—so no harm done.

She also taught me to milk the cow. If you've never done that, it's probably not so much a bucket list item. It's funny and fun to learn—for the first few minutes—but it gets old, quickly. Your face is plastered up against the cow and craned to one side. You can't see what you're doing or anything happening around you. And then there's the cow's tail swinging around hitting you. See—not a to-do item for most people. But as I remember, Grandma was scared of me being around the cows, and I was told to stay away from them. It would probably hurt if they stepped on me. But nope! When Ms. B went, I went too. And she never let anything happen to me.

Mr. F, I liked but was scared of. I don't know why. He never did or said anything I can remember to scare me. I think it was because he was always so calm and quiet. He didn't interact with me—that may have been it. But I think he was a good guy. And I think grown men of that time just didn't interact with children, especially ones that weren't theirs. I don't know.

Ms. B will show up again in stories to follow. She was very special to me. And she made GOOD biscuits!

MEMORY MOMENTS

I remember summer nights. Sometimes when it was too hot to sleep, I'd watch for and count the car lights on the bedroom wall. There weren't many cars on the road, especially at night. And they lit up just one upper-corner wall and ceiling area. Simple. Easy. It worked.

The Message in the Book

Grandma had the ugliest silver aluminum Christmas tree I think I've ever seen. They all looked alike, I know. But that one just stuck with me—whew. They were all the rage in the seventies. Remember those things? They were metal tubes. You stuck the limbs into the holes and bent them around to look like a real Christmas tree.

The tree was stored in a cardboard box with round paper sleeves for each limb. I think I hated the box it was stored in more than the tree—old, dirty box (from living in the attic) with brown paper sleeves. I just hated it. It's funny what you can fixate on sometimes.

But Grandma liked that tree. It was one of her first artificial trees.

We used to go cut one down for her, but she decided some time along the way she didn't want to "mess with" a live tree any more. So there.

If you ignored the tree, there were some good things about her decorations. She had some stuffed elves. Now, they are all the rage—the Elf on the Shelf. Grandma had some old ones that were a bit bigger than the ones you buy now. Hers weren't red. These were green or gold, and a couple had striped outfits.

The story, as I've learned it, is the elves were Santa's helpers. Little spies! They would move around the house and sit and watch children to report back any naughtiness to Santa. I remember Grandma telling me they were watching to make sure I was a good girl, but that's all she said about it. The story I hear today is more elaborate. And of course, people are doing odd and funny things with the elves for social media. All she did was move them around every week. And yes, I have the elves now.

One other Christmas tradition I didn't fully comprehend until I was forty years old was one of her gifts to me. Every year Grandma gave me a big story/picture book. Some were children's bible stories, some just nursery stories. But in each book, she hand wrote a message to me.

She knew—and noted it in a couple of them—I couldn't even read them yet. And she probably knew I wouldn't see them until much later. I knew there was writing in the books but never thought to go back and read it. Life moved on, and I just went right along with it until—I found them at a low point in my life. I was forty years old. Sitting in my office/junk room, I looked up and saw them on a bookshelf. I'd looked up there right at them hundreds of times before. I remember thinking to myself, "Those are the books Grandma gave me." And I had the overwhelming urge to get them down and look at them.

Then I remembered the message in each book. I read all of them. They hit home. I sat and cried for what seemed like hours. Grandma had passed by that time, and I was just hearing how much she loved me. Some of her messages brought a bit of light and hope into my world on that day. That wasn't the best year I'd ever had—I needed Grandma and she was there.

I've scattered some of her notes throughout this book. They were written to a little girl too small to read or understand them at the time. But they mean a *great* deal to me now.

CHRISTMAS NOTE FROM GRANDMA

Christmas sure wouldn't be very much without you. We love you more than anything in the "whole wide world."

Little baby Jesus was sent into this world to save us from our sins and to brighten the world. And I think all little boys and girls are sent to brighten things up. They all have a place, and no two are alike. If they were, there wouldn't be any reason for one of them to be here.

Ask Jesus to lead and guide you, and you will find your place.

MEMORY MOMENTS

You wouldn't think it, but there is a special kind of fear attached to corncribs. They're little rooms filled with ears of corn still in their husks. Grandma's was probably ten by ten feet. It was in the barn. The fear comes in when you're in the corncrib picking out ears of corn to take and eat—something moves, and the corn shifts. That's when you realize there are probably snakes living under the piles of corn. And you can't see them.

Diamond Rings and Salesmen

Grandma was a farmer's wife. All her friends were farmers' wives. By the time I was old enough to pay attention, they were more retired than anything. They spent way too much time and energy keeping up with other people's business. It was a small town, and everyone knew everyone else's business.

I was little—seven, eight, or nine years old. My grandfather had passed away, so Grandma had been a widow for a while at that point. My mother took Grandma's old diamond rings and traded them in for one solitaire diamond. Don't ask me why; I don't know. And I never asked.

Grandma wore it somewhere—where some of her friends saw it—and just so happened it was on her left-hand ring finger. "Where did you get that diamond?!" It was on from there. I wonder if she wore it there on purpose?

The next thing I knew, she was wearing it on her left-hand ring finger any time she went somewhere with her friends. Her friends *assumed* she had a boyfriend. Then they made the jump to him being a traveling salesman from Charlotte. I have no idea how they made those jumps. I really don't think she ever actually said anything—but I doubt she denied anything either.

These women became obsessed with catching Grandma with this man. They would park on the side of the road at the other end of the tobacco field and watch her house trying to see who was coming and going. All her neighbors were "on watch" for any strange cars. It was hysterical!

A few months passed. Grandma and I were at church. I got cornered by some of her friends. You know the type—somewhat nosy "church ladies" who do no wrong and have the right to know everything about everyone else. Don't misunderstand—these were Grandma's friends, and I liked most of them very much. But the stereotype is so obvious when I look back on it.

Let me set this up. They thought they knew something very "juicy" about Grandma—that she had a boyfriend who was a traveling salesman from Charlotte and that he was coming to visit her on weekends. They had been trying to catch this mysterious man at Grandma's house but never could. And now they had her young granddaughter cornered in church—alone.

I was taught well: do not lie, especially to adults and even more so to any of Grandma's friends! Can you see what's coming next?

I knew not to lie to these women. I also knew Grandma didn't have a boyfriend. Grandma had told me point blank not to tell anyone anything about the boyfriend or the ring. But I had grown up in an environment where all these women had some level of authority over me just because they were Grandma's friends, meaning they had the right to question me. And I was supposed to answer truthfully.

So you see my problem. At seven, eight, or nine years old, this was a serious problem!

"Jenny, tell us about your Grandma's boyfriend."

I couldn't tell them the truth. And I couldn't lie to them. I vividly remember going through the choices. *Then* I remembered what Grandma told me. I could tell them *that* truth: "Grandma told me not to tell anybody anything." Score one for me—I win! I didn't lie. And I didn't tell on Grandma.

About that time, Grandma walked up, disrupted the gathering, and ushered me out to the car to go home. Whew! She was grinning from ear to ear and told me she had seen and heard it all. I had done good.

In the car, I finally asked what was going on and why she was telling them this story. I don't remember the exact quotes, but it was something like this: She knew her friends didn't have enough to occupy their time. So when they all pounced on the ring the first time she wore it, all assuming on their own there was a story there she wasn't telling, she decided to indulge them a little bit and allowed their imaginations to run with it.

She hadn't said a whole lot, if anything. They never allowed her time to answer the original question about where she got the ring. So she decided to let them all take their thoughts out to wherever they wanted to go. She let them feed the story themselves until it finally caught up with me in church.

What she told me was that she and her friends spent too much time gossiping about other people and often let their imaginations carry the stories too far. She decided that first day to let them gossip about her for a while, so someone else could get a rest.

As you can imagine, that took some thought for me to figure out. I didn't know what gossiping was. I didn't really understand the whole lesson until years later, high school to be exact. That's when I realized what gossip really was and how much it could hurt someone.

It's so easy to believe anything you're told and then to tell it for fact, whether it's true or not. This one time with Grandma was fairly harmless. But think about how different it might have been if the woman in question was younger or had children. What if she had worked somewhere that frowned on a boyfriend coming to spend the weekend with her, like a church or religious school?

To this day, I try—but don't always succeed—not to gossip about people. Honestly, nothing anyone else does is really any of my business. And for the most part, I don't care. I have enough to do just to keep up with me!

Though, I will admit, I have been caught doing exactly what Grandma did. But on a smaller scale—no diamond rings or traveling salesmen here. There have been times I've overheard something someone has said about me, repeating what they've heard or making their own assumption. Sometimes it's fun to just let them think what they want and say what they want. Every single time, it works out in my favor to leave it alone and let them go. It always backfires on them. And I have a good laugh, mostly just quietly to myself.

Dogs in the Garden

Grandma always had multiple gardens going. The only time there wasn't something growing was winter: December to March.

She and her friends were funny. They all seemed to grow too much of one thing. So swapping was a big event all through the summer. We were always taking bushels of peas to someone and bringing back corn or tomatoes or something else. It was a neat system!

It also extended to my house. My mother and I went to Grandma's every Saturday. And during peak garden months, we'd come home with buckets of tomatoes, squash, and cucumbers—too much for our family to eat. So my mother would make up bags that I would carry to neighbors. It was fun—everyone seemed to enjoy Grandma's garden!

I loved Grandma's gardens. Even if I didn't eat the particular item we were picking and processing, it was peaceful and satisfying to go pick. We'd get to the fields just after sunrise, before the heat set in. And some days we were still there 'til about lunch. You picked until there was nothing left to pick. Then you'd spend the afternoon processing—shelling, washing, and putting up.

She had one small garden down in a hollow (a small valley, a hole). It was good soil and grew nice healthy plants. It was surrounded by woods. And snakes and other varmints! She did something odd in that garden. She would take old biscuits with her and throw them out into the garden. Hang with me here—this is good.

My uncle lived on the farm a couple fields away—a few hundred yards. But his dogs usually hung out at Grandma's house. When she went to this little garden, she'd call the dogs to go with her. And when she threw the biscuits out into the garden, they would take off running through the plants to find them.

Here's the smart part of this story: snakes and other varmints would hear the racket from the dogs and start moving out the other end of the garden away from the noise. So we could move in and pick without worrying so much about snakes in particular. Tell me—how smart is that! Really?

After picking everything available, we'd bring it all back to the house. My job, as youngest person there, was to start shelling. Grandma and my mother would process all the non-shellable things like tomatoes and cucumbers—get them washed and set out. Then everyone would end up in the yard shelling whatever beans or peas were picked.

Brag point here: I can flat shell me some peas and butterbeans! I do have a skill set there if I ever need one.

Sitting out in Grandma's yard, under those big shade trees with the breeze, was wonderful. The older I got the better it was. The only noises were the animals and chitchat of the people there. Occasionally a car would go by but nothing really big or noisy. Time just stopped. Nothing mattered but getting through the buckets of peas or beans. I'd just sit and shell, letting my mind wander until we were all done. Sometimes, now, I'd love to go back to that time and zone out for a few hours forgetting the stresses of my day.

Funny, I don't remember ever eating veggies out of cans from the grocery store until much later in life. We always had canned or frozen veggies. To this day I have a hard time eating grocery store canned veggies. I don't mean anything with that comment, but when you grow up eating out of your own garden, the tastes are very different and hard to get used to.

At one point I remember Grandma being very worried about my eating choices. I was moving to Charlotte with the company I worked for. That seemed to be a change in her thinking. Before, I was in Raleigh (in school) and was still coming home to get food from her gardens. Getting a "real" job and moving a little farther away upset her. She worried I would start eating junk and not the healthy food she grew.

She was right to some degree. I did go home quite a bit and get veggies from the gardens. As long as she was able to manage the gardens, I tried my best to fit in time to go help. And bring back goodies.

There was nothing like a big pot of Grandma's peas or beans! Just enough fatback or bacon grease to season them—whew that was *good* stuff! And then you'd eat on them for several days. I'll still cook a big pot and eat four or five meals off the pot. They get better each time you heat them up.

One final memory on this garden and shelling story: When you're shelling you use a big pan of some kind. You fill the pan with peas and shell right into the same pan. The hulls got thrown into a bucket and dumped. When your pan was done, all you had was the shelled peas or beans.

Grandma had a set of ugly, flower-patterned, round, metal pans. The smallest one was in her kitchen sink. The largest one wasn't used much. She usually ended up using the middle-sized one to shell into. When she passed, I wanted those pans. No one knew why; they're rusted and not really useful for anything.

But to me they were part of the memory. I don't use them. They live in a cabinet in my kitchen. And that's OK. I know they're there. And they remind me of easier, simpler times with a wonderful woman. It's a great way to detach from the stresses of the day and think back to a time when sitting in the yard shelling peas was the most important thing.

It's OK

Grandma's house was comfortable, freeing. A place you could be yourself and not worry so much about being perfect or what someone else expected of you. I noticed after Grandma passed "it's OK" was how she lived, especially with me. She didn't say it very often; it was just the general atmosphere.

One easy example is living on a farm. If you'll imagine with me, farms are dirty places. Between the gardens and the animals, especially chicken houses—whew—there was always some form of non-clean happening. You did not wear "good clothes" at Grandma's. You couldn't go to the garden or tend the animals in "good clothes," so there was no need to have them on.

To this day, I have different sets of clothes. When I come home for the day, I'll change clothes. The clothes I wear to work or to go out get put away. I wear sweats or shorts or something very comfortable and easy to wash around the house. That way I don't have to worry about getting something on my clothes or worry too much about the animal hair I live with. That definitely came from Grandma's.

You could be dirty at Grandma's. She didn't fuss about dirty clothes or hands or faces—until meal times. The only hard and fast rule was to leave your "farm shoes" outside or out on the porch. Any footwear you wore to the chicken house or out in the field was automatically left outside. We were some shoe-changing people! Easy for me—I was usually barefoot anyway.

Funny aside: My dad was a mechanic. He took his boots off as soon as he walked in the door. So I had two sides of the family teaching me to take my shoes off at the door. Works for me! I *love* being barefoot. To this day I hate wearing shoes in the house. Everyone laughs at me—my sneakers and one pair of flip-flops live at the door to slide into when I go out. Barefoot Baby—that's how I roll! Or is it walk?

So back to the point. It was also OK if you didn't like something, butterbeans for example. No, I don't like butterbeans! And it was OK that the furniture didn't match, the plates didn't match, and the sheets and bedspreads weren't perfectly coordinated sets. You see my point.

Grandma's house was a place to live and experience and learn. It was clean and neat and comfortable. I didn't have to worry about breaking that "special" piece of furniture or walking across that expensive rug. At Grandma's you could be yourself, and it was OK.

Everything at Grandma's was handled that way. A broken glass: it's OK; we'll use another one. Accidently picked a tomato before it was fully ripe: it's OK; we'll set it up in the window. She seemed to have a way with letting little things not become big things. Just handle it and move on.

I catch myself doing that same thing with people close to me. When they panic or get stressed over something I can see is a small thing, I'm the one saying, "It's OK; we got this."

I do that with clients as well. For what I do for them, there isn't much they can mess up that I can't fix. I have a couple of clients who like to do things for themselves. Great! But every once in a while, they'll do something careless or forget how to do something correctly. Then they call me in a panic because they messed it up. "It's OK. I'll fix it." I do, and all is right with the world again.

Grandma's sense of calm and acceptance that "it's OK" was a wonderful gift. I'm very glad she shared it with me. It *is* OK.

Miss Gladys

For a couple years Grandma was in craft overload. She was taking classes with some of her friends. I'm assuming—it was close to just after Granddaddy passed—she was trying some new things, getting out of the house. I get it.

One thing she learned was to crochet. She learned how to make all those little "homey" things around the house. She had a toilet paper cover on every roll. There were soap covers, yarn doilies, and other things with pompoms all over the place. I had several toboggans with pompoms on top. Note here: my fine hair is *not* conducive to yarn toboggans.

She finally graduated to afghans. For non-crochet people, those are blankets. Those I *loved* and still have a couple she made for me.

She'd use any yarn she could find on sale somewhere. We'd make runs to the stores and buy whatever yarn they had on sale. She didn't care much about colors, which created some interesting patterns. And she'd use a skein until it ran out—didn't matter if it was on a row end or not—then start a new skein or even a new color.

I have one afghan in particular that is incredibly "un-pretty." It has odd colors, one of which is neon orange, and starts and stops of colors in odd places. I *loved* that afghan. I didn't care about pretty—she made it for me, and I thought it was perfect.

Then she taught me. I love to crochet still. It's calming and a great way to zone out and de-stress, like pea shelling. I even use her favorite needle in most projects. But I've learned how to make all those little scrap skeins and all the different colors look a little better.

But that's not all she learned to do.

One day, Grandma decided to make me a doll. She'd heard about Cabbage Patch dolls. That they were all the rage. But she was not going to pay the going rate for one. Very happy about that! Her class was making dolls, and she decided she'd make me one.

Note here: I did not play with dolls and have not, to my memory, ever played with dolls. I had a Barbie but don't remember doing much with her. I don't even know where she is. And personally, I thought Cabbage Patch dolls were the dumbest looking and ugliest things I'd ever seen—at the time. I was in middle school or junior high I think—lots of things were "dumb" and "ugly" at that age.

But Grandma didn't care. She made me a doll. She—the doll—did not look like a Cabbage Patch doll, thankfully! Her name was Miss Gladys. I couldn't hide the fact that I did not like Miss Gladys. And even so, she—the doll—became a running joke in the house. Grandma and my mother delighted in constantly asking me about her—where she was and if I was going to take her to college.

I have to give Grandma much overdue credit. She tried to do something for a teenaged girl who had not yet learned the art of gracious acceptance of a gift she didn't want. Grandma didn't let the fact that I was openly hostile about the doll kill her joy. She had made it for me and was proud of that.

As I'm writing this I think I really do owe her an apology for my attitude. It was a sweet thing to do, and I completely messed it up. I did take Miss Gladys home—Grandma made me. And I think she's still at my parents' house. The last time I saw her, she was sitting in a rocking chair in what was my bedroom.

And I finally learned the lesson. Gifts are given—and accepted—without judgment or scorn. I've learned to appreciate the thought as much or more than the gift itself.

CHRISTMAS NOTE FROM GRANDMA

I just can't let Christmas go by without giving you something with a lasting value.

The love of Christ for you is lasting and will hold up, never wears out or grows old. Cars, dolls, books, Mickey Mouse, and even "Zips" are all nice, but they are of a worldly nature and will not last; they grow old and soon wear out, but Christ's love for you never grows old or wears out. He is patient and loves you no matter what you do. He is hurt when you disobey him, but in his patient and kind way, he tries to guide and direct you; he is always ready to forgive you and take you back into his fold if you ask him to forgive you.

We are all his children, and he loves you as your parents love you. When you get to be a big girl and disobey them, it will hurt them, but if they try to live like Christ and be a Christian, they are ready to forgive you and help you all they can.

We all love you; you are a "dear little girl."

Grandma Lied to Her Best Friend

This is one of my favorite "Grandma stories." I was little—somewhere in the seven, eight, or nine year range. Someone dropped a puppy off at Grandma's house. He was sweet and playful but ugly. Wow, he was an ugly little dog. Obviously, he was an odd mixed mutt of some kind. Grandma did not want another dog—any other dog.

"Jenny, let's go visit Ms. G tonight."

Ms. G was one of Grandma's best friends. I loved her! She was "neat," you know. And we would go over and "visit." That meant they would sit in the kitchen and talk (or gossip) and I would hang around and watch TV or play with something till they were done. Don't laugh—that was "high fun" at the time!

This night, we took the puppy. And we stopped at the front of the house. Grandma knew no one would be looking out the front since the front of the house was closed off. "Jenny, put that puppy outside on the ground, and we'll drive around."

I sat the puppy out, and we pulled away. Watching, I saw him following us. We got out of the car, and naturally, the puppy was right there. Ms. G was coming out the backdoor waving.

Grandma made a big fuss about the puppy. "G, where did you get such a pretty little puppy? He's precious." She lied to her best friend!

I just kept quiet—about to die to laugh.

Ms. G said, "Oh my gosh, what an ugly little puppy! Who would drop him off here!?" It never occurred to her we brought him.

We spent the next couple hours there—them sitting in the kitchen gossiping and me outside playing with the puppy.

Back in the car, Grandma apparently felt the need to explain what she'd done. "Jenny, I don't hate the little dog. I just don't want a dog to take care of. Ms. G has several and can easily take him in. But we don't need to tell her who dropped him off."

"Yes, ma'am," was all I could get out. We laughed all the way back home—and laughed for years to come. It was our private joke.

I don't know if she ever told Ms. G about the puppy. And I don't know what happened to him. I have a vague memory of him being there for a couple years. Most of her family lived on or around their farm, and there were always kids and dogs moving around. I know he was cared for. I hope he was happy.

Tobacco Worms

Grandma lived on a tobacco farm. That's what they were growing as a cash crop by the time I was born. The house was surrounded by tobacco fields.

When a field was ready, we were "called to the barn." That day—very early—we all showed up at the barn. Most of the men went out to the field to start priming the first trailer load. The women set up the stringer and got ready. The stringer was a conveyor belt machine with a large sewing needle and twine at the head to tie, or sew, the tobacco onto the stick.

Understand, there are dozens of procedures and "ways" of putting in a barn of tobacco. This is generally how we did it. So I don't want to hear any noise about "how it's done" somewhere else.

The guys in the field put the tobacco on an open-sided trailer with the stalks pointed out. The full trailer was then backed into its spot at the barn. Beside the trailer were three women standing between it and the stringer. They would reach around, grab a handful of the tobacco, and lay it on the stringer. Over and over.

The first woman on the outside would lay the first row of tobacco. The second would fill that row and lay a stick in the correct place near the stalk ends of the leaves and start filling the top row. The third woman, closest to the wall, would fill the top row and make sure the needle sewed the string correctly.

Just inside the door, there was a man who would grab that stick of tobacco and lift it off the stringer and up to another man standing up on poles that ran side to side the width of the barn. The tobacco sticks were hung on those poles—like clothes in a closet.

Covering the floor, there were heaters. When the tobacco was hung, the heaters would run continually for several days and dry the leaves. It was very hot and humid in the barn! I did *not* like going in the barn during the drying process.

My part, as a little person, was multifaceted. The talent I had was amazing! The main function of all my "jobs" was to keep me occupied and busy. I didn't know that at the time, of course, and thought I was the most important worker there. Grandma told me I was.

I was allowed to go out on the tractor occasionally. Mostly to sit in the seat and make sure the tractor ran straight, which meant just sit and watch. Looking back, I wasn't driving. The wheels were in ruts, and the tractor was barely moving. I doubt I could have turned it out of the ruts if I tried. And my uncle had the throttle locked at the speed he wanted—slow.

Another important job was moving the tobacco from the outside side of the trailer to the inside side, so the women on the stringer didn't have to reach for it. I would sit up in the middle of the rows, and as the tobacco on the inside side would go down, I'd just lift the tobacco from the outside side and flip it over onto the inside side with the stalks facing out. That job was actually useful and kinda fun.

Here's the really "fun" part. Ms. B was always on the inside nearest the needle and the wall, meaning she was pretty much trapped in that spot. I loved Ms. B dearly. She was deathly afraid of the large neon green worms (caterpillars) that lived on the tobacco plants—"tobacco worms." They were usually the size of an adult's index finger and an odd neon (without the glow) green color. Harmless but ugly!

Naturally, I just had to throw them on Ms. B when I could. She would scream and jump around like someone had set her on fire. I thought it was hysterical! But remember, little people find things funny when most adults don't. She never scolded me, but Grandma did. I couldn't help it. It was fun!

Another job I had, the one mainly to keep me busy, was to wander around in the barn and pick up any leaves that had fallen down from the hanging sticks. Occasionally, leaves wouldn't get sewn in completely, and they'd fall. "We do not waste leaves." Didn't like that job—it was hot and dark in the barn.

Filling a barn usually took most of the day. We'd start right after daylight and finish early afternoon. Five or six guys in the field, three women on the stringer, two or three men in the barn, and me doing odd jobs. I was the only child in the group—and in the family at the time.

After the barn was put in, it was time to wash up. That was easier said than done! The guys in the field wore long sleeves and long pants. It took me years to figure that out. Here's why. You walk down the row of tobacco plants. You pull the leaves off the bottom of the plant with one hand and sling them under the other arm. So when you have an arm full, it looks like you're carrying a package or something under that one arm.

Tobacco leaves a sticky tar all over you. So any bare skin will collect the tar. That mess does NOT come off with a simple washing or wiping. It's sticky and rough, and it's on for at least a week until it wears off. *Unless* you use lye soap. You'll get rid of the tobacco tar and about three layers of skin. Now you understand why the guys in the fields always had on long sleeves in that 95-degree, straight-sun-shining-down-on-them heat. Whew.

Lye soap will take tobacco tar off, but it's rough stuff. It'll take hide, hair, and all! Ms. B made homemade lye soap every year. And Grandma always had a shoebox full of that stuff to use for bathing. It was fine for normal bathing or handwashing. I've taken many baths with lye soap. Personally, I would not recommend it. Sorry, but there it is.

I have to admit, my favorite part of the whole day was going with Granddaddy to the gas station in town to get drinks and nabs. Nabs, for you people who don't know, are usually Lance crackers. He was too sick by that time to work at the barn. So we'd go late morning and get a case of soft drinks and a couple cases of nabs to have for a break. "We don't stop for lunch. We'll eat enough to hold us then have a good supper." When we got back, and when the next trailer load would come in, we all took a break under the apple tree.

I'm sure me going with him was more to give me something to do and give them a break from having me around. I hope he enjoyed having me go with him. As I mentioned before, I don't have actual memories of him, but I have impressions of memories from stories I've heard. I remember, vividly, putting in tobacco—though probably from later years.

I've had "jobs" as long as I can remember. The authoritative adults in my world thought children should do chores (jobs). And it wasn't always for pay for those jobs—things needed to be done, and it was my job to do them. End of discussion.

But I love when people ask me what my first "job" was, meaning my first paying job! My first paycheck was for a tobacco barn. Granddaddy paid me $15 dollars—and, yes, it was a check. I think my mother had him do that. I remember taking my check to the bank and opening my first account with it. I was an official "Tiger Club" member! I think I still have that bank book somewhere.

MEMORY MOMENTS

I love buckets. I think the bucket "thing" started with my dad. He worked in a place that always had big, five-gallon buckets left over. He brought them home. We had buckets everywhere. Most of them ended up at Grandma's. We used them to carry stuff from the gardens. For some reason, far back in my pea-brain, I equate the buckets to Grandma's. I still love buckets.

Good Pop on the Rear End

Point of fact: Grandma believed in spankings and switchings. She would make me and my cousins go get our own switches off a yellow bell bush in her front yard. That's a horrible thing—when you're about to be switched, going to pick out the switch that will be used on your own rear end. And if we picked the wrong switch, we would have to go back and get another one. That's just painful!

    I don't remember ever being switched, and I don't remember going to get them very often. Most of the time, she would make us go get the switch and come back. By that time we'd be crying and trying to think of any way out of it. Then she'd ask questions about us knowing what we did and if we had learned anything. You know the questions parents ask. That was usually "enough"—you know. We knew the threat could and would be carried out. And we knew to *not* do whatever it was again. Grandma was not to be messed with. What she said was law!

But that's how it was with her grandchildren. She had the inherent right as our grandparent to discipline us. The other side of this story—disciplining other people's children—would probably cause problems today.

Grandma and her friends felt they had the right and obligation to "police" and discipline all the children in their sphere of influence. And for Grandma, the sphere included any children around her at any time and in any place.

When I was little, it was nothing for Grandma to stop a mother in public and point out that her children needed "controlling." I've seen her on several occasions even offer to dole out the spanking herself—right there and right then. That was a different time. *None* of the mothers ever complained or balked. Most of the time they thanked her for noticing, and the spanking was handled on the spot.

I was even subjected once—ONE TIME. That was all it took. I was little. Grandma and I had been shopping for a while. It was the last store, and I was almost at my limit. Understand, I was very controlled when I was little. I did *not* act up in public and did *not* do anything Grandma or my mother would be embarrassed by.

On that day, I was getting fussy. Tired. Little people get tired. I had one weak moment and whined about something. Oh no! Grandma was not having it. She grabbed my arm, pulled me around, and gave me one "good" hard pop right on the rear end and sat me down right where I was. I was so stunned I didn't make a sound. And by the time I got my wits back, I knew better than to make a sound. Remember that quote "cry and I'll give you something to cry about"? She went on about her business, and the incident was over.

I remember looking around and seeing other adults nodding in approval and giving me that "you deserved that" look. The pop didn't hurt. The shock of getting it—and without any warning or notice—is what made the impression.

A little later Grandma said, "Jenny, you know why you got popped, don't you?" I did know. I had whined, and that was not happening in her world.

That's the way it was when I was little. *Any* adult around you had the right to dole out minor punishment and had the obligation to make the parents handle their children in public. I did *not* cut up or act out—at all—especially in public. That's just the way it was. Period!

All of the adults in Grandma's circle had the right to tear my hind end up if I needed it. But the bigger fear was they would tell her I was misbehaving. *That* would have been even worse. At that point, I would be not only misbehaving but also embarrassing Grandma. 'Cause they *knew* I'd been raised better and should know better!

We, as children, didn't get bribed, begged, or warned. There were rules, and we were expected to know them and abide by them. Out in public, we were also not allowed out of arm's reach of the adult we came with. If I was in a store with either Grandma or my mother, I knew to stay within arm's reach. I wasn't sent to the toy section or told to "go play" in a store. Oh no. "You stay with me, do not touch anything, and do not wander off."

Kinda wish there were more people like Grandma around when I go into some public places now! I can't imagine, when I was little, being allowed to run wild in a store or to scream bloody murder just because I wanted to. I admit it—I am a believer in spankings. Maybe not switchings so much and certainly not beatings. But a good pop on the rear end when you're little can solve a lot of problems later on.

MEMORY MOMENTS

I had a few toys that lived at Grandma's: a large, silver (plated) serving spoon, a round knife sharpener, and a bag of wooden clothespins. It's amazing what you can do with a little imagination!

Saving a Missing Tooth

Grandma's house was the sick house. When I was too sick to go to school for more than a day, I went to stay with Grandma. She let me do what I wanted, eat what I wanted, and sleep when I wanted and with no schedules or requirements. If you had to be sick, that was the place to be.

As I remember, my kindergarten year had a lot of sick time at Grandma's. That year, we all (in my class) went through chicken pox, measles, and mumps! I remember overhearing Grandma telling my mother at some point, "Well, she's getting them all done and over with now." I've learned—after many years—it was probably a good thing to "get them done and over with."

During sick days at Grandma's, she got my "sick cot" out. It was one of those old, aluminum-frame, folding cots with the springs across under the mattress. The mattress was an ugly green with white stripes. Remember those things? Whew, they were rough to look at—and rougher to sleep on—but perfect for a sick little person.

She would set it up in the middle of the den. Remember the den is pretty much the center and focal point of the house. In the winter, it was right beside the stove for heat. In the summer, it was in the cross breeze from open windows on each side of the house. I was also right in the middle of all the activity. The TV (black and white, with all three channels!) was there. The kitchen was the next room, and the bathroom just down the hall on the other side of the stove. The hall was only about five feet long. And I could just lie down and go to sleep whenever I wanted.

I think for her it was easier too. I was already an independent child. As long as I had something to do or to occupy me, I was easy to deal with. Being in the den, she didn't have to make me go to bed or keep up with where I was. She could just leave me to whatever I wanted to do, go about her business, and not have to "babysit." Smart woman!

The downsides of being sick at Grandma's were castor oil and milk of magnesia. WOW, that was rough stuff. I don't remember the taste or sensations of the castor oil. But I can still—to this day, to this minute—gag on the memory of that big ol' tablespoon of thick, chalky milk of magnesia. Good gosh! If you've ever had it, you will not ever forget it.

There was one particular sick day that left an impression and let me know just how much Grandma loved me. Somewhere around the fourth or fifth grade I had a retainer for a missing tooth. I had just gotten it and was getting used to it. And I *knew* not to lose or damage it in any way, shape, or form.

Sick to my stomach, Grandma told me to go throw up. Sounded like a great idea, so off I went. What I forgot to do was take my retainer out first. Naturally, it dropped into the commode with everything else. I panicked!

Sick, tired, and afraid of what my mother would say about losing my new retainer, I went to Grandma in tears. I just knew life was over and all was lost! Oh the drama.

But Grandma did something that just amazed me—something only a grandma would do. She stuck her hand in all that mess and pulled my retainer out. She washed it off and handed it back to me. "Honey, it's OK. Let's just put it up and don't worry about wearing it until you feel better."

You cannot imagine how much that meant to me! Grandma didn't fuss at me for allowing it to fall out—for not thinking ahead enough to take it out first. She didn't fuss at me for not reaching in to get it myself. She recognized I was "compromised" by being sick and not thinking as clearly as I normally would have been. She just handled my crisis. She not only made my mistake "go away" but also gave me permission to not worry about it. Grandma rocked!

CHRISTMAS NOTE FROM GRANDMA

Jesus was sent into the world to teach the people about God and his love for them. Everyone was sent into this world for a purpose, and if you ask God's guidance, you will find yours. You have already brought a lot of sunshine into our home. We love you with all our hearts.

You are a "dear little girl."

Interrogation!

Grandma had fields and fields of peas. Peas everywhere! I love the Dixie Lea peas she planted. Basically, they are small black-eyed peas—good flavor. Pea picking and pea shelling were staple activities at Grandma's. If you were there during certain weeks in the summer, part of your day involved one or both activities.

Funny now as I remember, the women did the picking and shelling and processing. Granddaddy and my uncle (the men) were in charge of field work—plowing and planting. I never saw either of them pick or shell one stinking pea.

I remember many days sitting in the back yard in a folding yard chair or in the swing shelling peas. Occasionally a pea would shoot out onto the ground. There were usually chickens wandering around in the yard. They would all race around finding and eating them. It was fun to watch!

But you just tune out—at least I would. The adults, Grandma and my mother usually, were talking about whatever they were talking about, and I would just let my mind wander. It would be a great way to destress today.

I also remember one day in particular. I took my husband-to-be to meet her. He had never picked a pea in his life; I warned him. Grandma was ready. "Let's go to the pea field." Now remember, the men in her world didn't pick peas. We walked down the back road, hundred yards or so, not far.

I told Grandma he had never picked peas. She only grinned and said, "We'll teach him." That turned out to be the first test—that he would even try to pick peas. He passed!

Arriving at the pea field, she said, "Jenny, you start over there. Lee, you come with me." She intentionally separated me from their conversation. All I could do was hope he "did OK." I knew he would. His running joke is he's "God's gift" to dogs and old women.

I learned on the ride home she used the opportunity to question him. Interrogation! Apparently, she taught him how to pick the peas, then started asking questions. He said it wasn't bad, and he understood she wanted to make sure he was "OK" for me.

I just hee-hawed as he was telling me about his pea-picking experience. He has not picked a pea since and has no intention of picking another pea. But he will tell the story in a heartbeat. I think he enjoyed the lesson. He liked Grandma. And Grandma liked him!

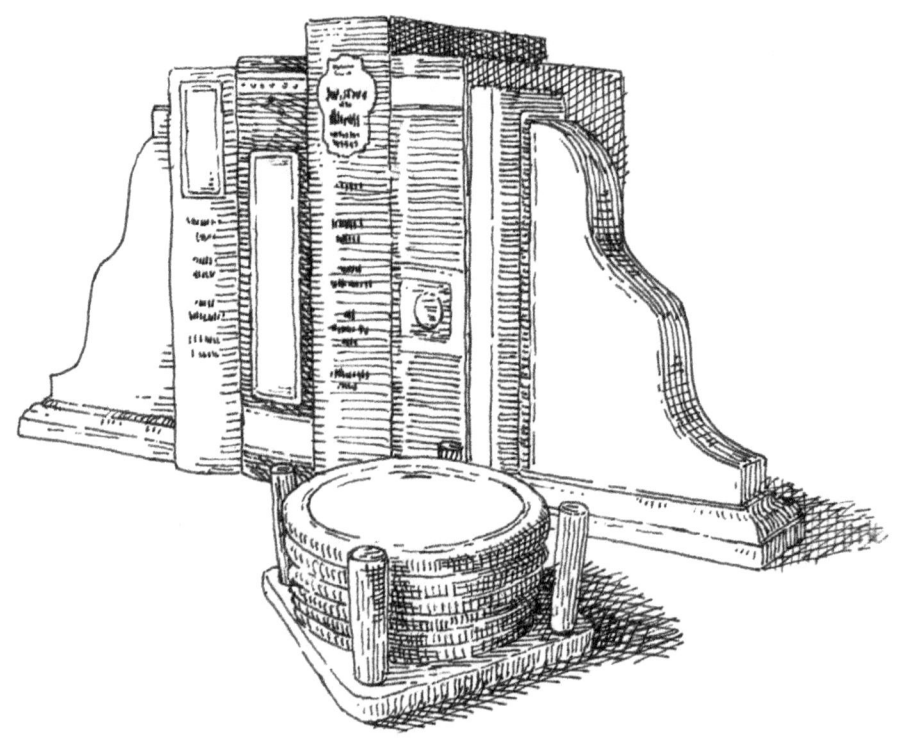

Free Snob

To this day I really don't like the word "free." And I think it started with Grandma—good, bad or otherwise!

When I was little, the furniture store in the next town over would send out sales flyers. In them was a coupon for a free thing—coasters, bookends, or some other small knick-knack. You had to bring in the coupon to get the free item. And there was a limit of one per person, per trip. That's how I got involved.

Grandma and my mother would get three flyers and make me take one of the coupons in to get the free item. And when you're eight or nine years old, walking through a furniture store with a coupon for a free item is incredibly uncomfortable. They *know* you aren't going to buy any furniture. And they *know* an adult has sent you. I remember the people at the service desk where you redeemed the coupons picking at me. I hated redeeming those coupons!

Funny part about the whole thing—these weren't things she ever used. She would put them in a closet or in the spare bedroom to collect dust. I asked her a couple times why she wanted them. "I'll give them as Christmas presents." What!? That didn't even make sense. Everyone Grandma gave gifts too would have received the same sales flyer and redeemed the coupon for themselves. As far as I know, she never did give or use any of that stuff. I don't know what happened to all of it.

"Free" is only free if you want it and will use it. Otherwise it's a waste of time. Those experiences turned me into a "free snob." Maybe this is a good thing!

I have a couple of examples of "free" wasting my time. Understand, these are my opinions. If you like free, go forth and enjoy! You can have mine.

"Free with purchase" deals: I've had more makeup bags and samples given to me just because when I needed to buy makeup, they were giving them away as "free with purchase." They went straight into the trash. I didn't need them. I didn't want them. But arguing with the ladies at the sales counter in the store is a horrible experience to begin with, especially for something so silly. Try telling one of "those ladies" you don't want the free gift. Go ahead; try it. Those women get upset!

Another one I just *love* (or not): "free to try." One guy called me at work a few years ago when printer cartridges were a big thing. He went through his whole pitch and asked me how many cartridges I wanted to have shipped.

"None."

"But ma'am, these cartridges are free for you to use. All we ask is you return the empty cartridges with your next order."

"With my next order? Then they aren't free."

And I don't want your cartridges anyway.

OK, there is built-in guilt there. I'm one of those people—if I don't want to use your product and have no intention of buying from you in the future, I don't want the guilt of having taken your free stuff with your assumption that I would then purchase. I just don't want to mess with it. I'd rather tell you no, and we both move on. Saves me a whole lot of aggravation.

Another version of that "free to try" thing is try it free then cancel if you don't want it.

"Ma'am, we will set up service for two months for free. If you're not happy you can call and cancel the service."

OK, wait! That is not what I consider free! If I have to *do* something and then argue with another salesperson to end the "free" service, then it's costing me time and energy. Besides, if I don't want that service to begin with, having it for free for two months is not a good deal for me.

That whole try-it-for-free thing drives me nuts. If I'm already a customer (I was in the service example), then reward my loyalty with something I already use. Give me a discount for two months on my regular bill or something like that. Those very thinly veiled attempts to get me to buy something I'm not already getting are just tacky. It's bad customer service and leaves me, personally, with a bad impression of the company as a whole.

I know—I'm being a little picky about the whole thing. But I really think "free" is overrated! For "free" to be of value, it has to be something I want or need to begin with. If I wouldn't pay money for it on my own, I don't want it for free either. That does sound a little warped now that I say it out loud.

But we are a society driven by getting something for free. I'll pass. Most of the time I do better without the free offers. Or at least I feel like I do better 'cause then I don't have the hassle of dealing with whatever it was. I feel the same way about coupons for things I wouldn't buy to begin with. But that's a whole other story.

See—FREE snob!

I guess I can blame—or is it give credit to?—Grandma for this hang-up I have with "free." That furniture store is still a thing of nightmares.

OK, full disclaimer here: I am NOT talking about gifts from friends or clients. I've received a lot of gifts—things I didn't want. I've learned, especially after Miss Gladys, to be gracious and accept them. So free from gifts is a good thing!

After-Christmas Sales

OK, I know this is a sore spot for some of my friends. I am one of very few females who truly have NO desire to just "go shopping" for no particular reason. I do not live for shopping or shoes or pocketbooks. When I go shopping, I go get what I want and leave. So we'll get that out of the way right now.

One exception: I can spend all day, any day, in a bookstore!

Having said that. Grandma and I differ on this one point. She *loved* a good sale. She loved "free" too, but I talked about that earlier.

She had several pocketbooks and—for that era—enough shoes for any occasion. She was one of those people who would change her pocketbook to match her outfit and her shoes for the season. I thought it was a hoot. For someone who lived on a farm and didn't really "go out" that much or need to be dressed all that nicely, she was all over a good shoe sale!

Aside here: at this moment I have four pairs of sneakers, two pairs of black heels, one pair of flip-flops, and one pair of fuzzy warm house shoes (for winter). That's it! That's all I need! And I carry *one* pocketbook all year, every day I need to carry one. It is a name brand. But when you carry the same bag for seventeen years, you get your money's worth out of it. I carried my last pocketbook almost every day for two months shy of seventeen years. The shoulder strap finally broke. That's the only reason I retired it. Just so you understand the differences between Grandma and me on this point.

Grandma and my mother both loved a good sale, especially on clothes and shoes. Clothes shopping was and is the bane of my existence on days when it's necessary. When I was little, like most children then, they picked out all my clothes, told me to try them on, and decided what I liked. I had very few choices in clothing until I was in high school.

Saturdays that weren't garden days were shopping days. Used to kill me—we'd hit all the sales with sales papers in hand. To this day I detest those sales papers! And anything with a limit—yep—I got to buy my limited number of those items as well. I was a third person, and if they were rung up separately, it counted. And of course the cashiers always picked on me. What is it with employees at counters picking on kids? The furniture store people did too.

Clothes shopping was especially painful or maybe just boring for me. They were funny—they'd oohhh and aaahhh over things, then try stuff on forever. Well, it seemed like forever to me, a little person with nothing to do. And remember, I had to stay right with them—was not allowed to wander around on my own.

Another funny here: Grandma shopped ahead. At the after-Christmas sales, she'd buy clothes for people for gifts for next Christmas. She'd buy half of what she was going to give me with me right there. I'd try it on, she'd get a larger size, and she was done with her list! I'd forget all about it until next Christmas. Yes, I remembered them—I've seen these before. She saved money and half the stress was already gone.

But that's the way it was. She didn't have a lot of money but loved to find and take advantage of a good sale. I get it.

To this day, I rarely shop at all. And I usually don't even pay attention to sales. If I need something I'll go get it—at the best price I can find. If it's something big, like my refrigerator, I might wait and watch for the next appliance sale. But even then, I'm going to get what I want or need, and that's it. I'm an easy customer.

MEMORY MOMENTS

I remember my first—and last—taste of chewing tobacco. We were putting in a barn of tobacco, and I was out on the tractor—just sitting up in the seat. Apparently I was bugging my uncle about his chewing tobacco. He decided to shut me up by giving me some. He did not tell me I wasn't supposed to swallow the juice. Oh my gosh. That was nasty stuff! And out in that ninety-five-plus degree heat I was just as sick as I could be by the time we got back to the barn. Whew! I've not wanted any since. Lesson learned.

Meanness

Grandma's theory: if you aren't bleeding or violently sick, if nothing has been cut off, it's probably just "meanness" trying to work its way out. What? OK, hang in with me. This is a hard one until it clicks. But once it does, it's fun!

Remember, Grandma was a farmer's wife. And in her world, you didn't run to the doctor or drugstore for every little cut, scrape, or sniffle. Home remedies were widely used and accepted for most ailments or illnesses. If you weren't truly sick or hurt, you got up and went back to your business, which on a farm was usually work.

Your knee hurts—walk it off. Your head hurts—take something, go lay down for a while, then go back to work. Your stomach hurts—if you can throw up, do that and go back to work. If not, milk of magnesia was the solution. Whew, nasty stuff! You get my point.

So I think she created the "meanness" explanation as a way to explain to me why she didn't run to the doctor for every little thing or even allow herself to be sick. She didn't like being down. She had stuff to do and no time to be sick. It also took some of the seriousness out—it made it a little funnier and easier to deal with. It's a little warped, but when you think it through, it works.

When I was little and sick, I just stayed on my "sick cot" and allowed whatever it was to work its way out. She would give me whatever home remedy she thought was needed until I was better. As I got older, with minor things, I learned the same lesson—deal with it and move on.

To this day, I really have to be *bad* sick to not get on with my day. I may go a little slower than normal, but I still get on with it. Just because I don't feel good, doesn't mean things don't need to be done.

One note here: I have had a few headaches take me down. For those of you with migraines, I have all empathy and understanding of your pain. Take all the downtime and do whatever you need to do to get past them. WOW, those things are tough!

Back to Grandma. It's tricky with children. Sometimes you can't tell, and the only indicator is temperature. If my temperature would get too high, she'd take me to Dr. R, the only doctor in town. He had to be 180 years old at the time. That's the only thing I remember about him.

But I do remember hearing on one trip, "It's just a cold. She'll be fine. Keep her warm and keep fluids in her and let it run its course." No meds, no shots, nothing but common sense—time tested advice.

That same philosophy carried into my house with my parents. You didn't go to the doctor unless you really needed to. And I was (and am still) very lucky to not need to go very often.

Funny side story here: if I was sick, which really wasn't often, my dad would bring me a Mountain Dew. Honestly, that usually helped my upset stomach if nothing else. I've learned now, after all these years, it was the carbonation that helped—burping with a purpose. But at the time, that Mountain Dew was a miracle cure only Daddy knew.

So let me carry this back around to Grandma's theory—meanness. Now when I'm sick or have something minor going on, people ask about it: "Jenny, did you go to the doctor? What are you taking/doing to get better?" My answer is usually, "It's just meanness that needs to get out." People who know me will laugh and offer suggestions as to curing my exact meanness.

For people who don't know me well and aren't in my inner circle, it's an easy way of not answering the questions without flat-out insulting them. Most people don't need to know if I've been to the doctor or what I'm doing about it. They usually just turn and walk away.

But I've also taken Grandma's definition of "meanness" to a broader, more fun scale. Example: if you're having one of those days where you drop everything or have general clumsiness happening, I call that meanness. Same thing with hiccups or sneezing. Some of my friends have even started responding with what they think their meanness was. "Yep, I was too nice to that person."

It makes the clumsiness easier to deal with and the hiccups less embarrassing. And then no one feels the need to explain or apologize. Deal with it and move on. Works for me!

CHRISTMAS NOTE FROM GRANDMA

When we think of Christmas, we must think of the real meaning of Christmas, the birth of our Lord and Savior Jesus Christ. By believing in him and having faith in him, we are saved from our sins. Sometimes I think we forget this.

We get so involved with things, presents, and go to a lot of expense when it really isn't necessary.

Don't get me wrong—presents and Santa Claus are fine, so long as we don't strain ourselves with them. I don't think our Savior would like that. We don't find happiness in things. It's what's in the heart that counts.

You are growing up to be a fine young lady. And we are real proud of you. And I know from seeing you in the Christmas play, you are a natural born leader. So just "stay as sweet as you are." We love you very much.

The gift of love is the best gift of all. Like the little drummer boy who had no gift to offer the baby Jesus, but he could play his drum for him. The gift of love.

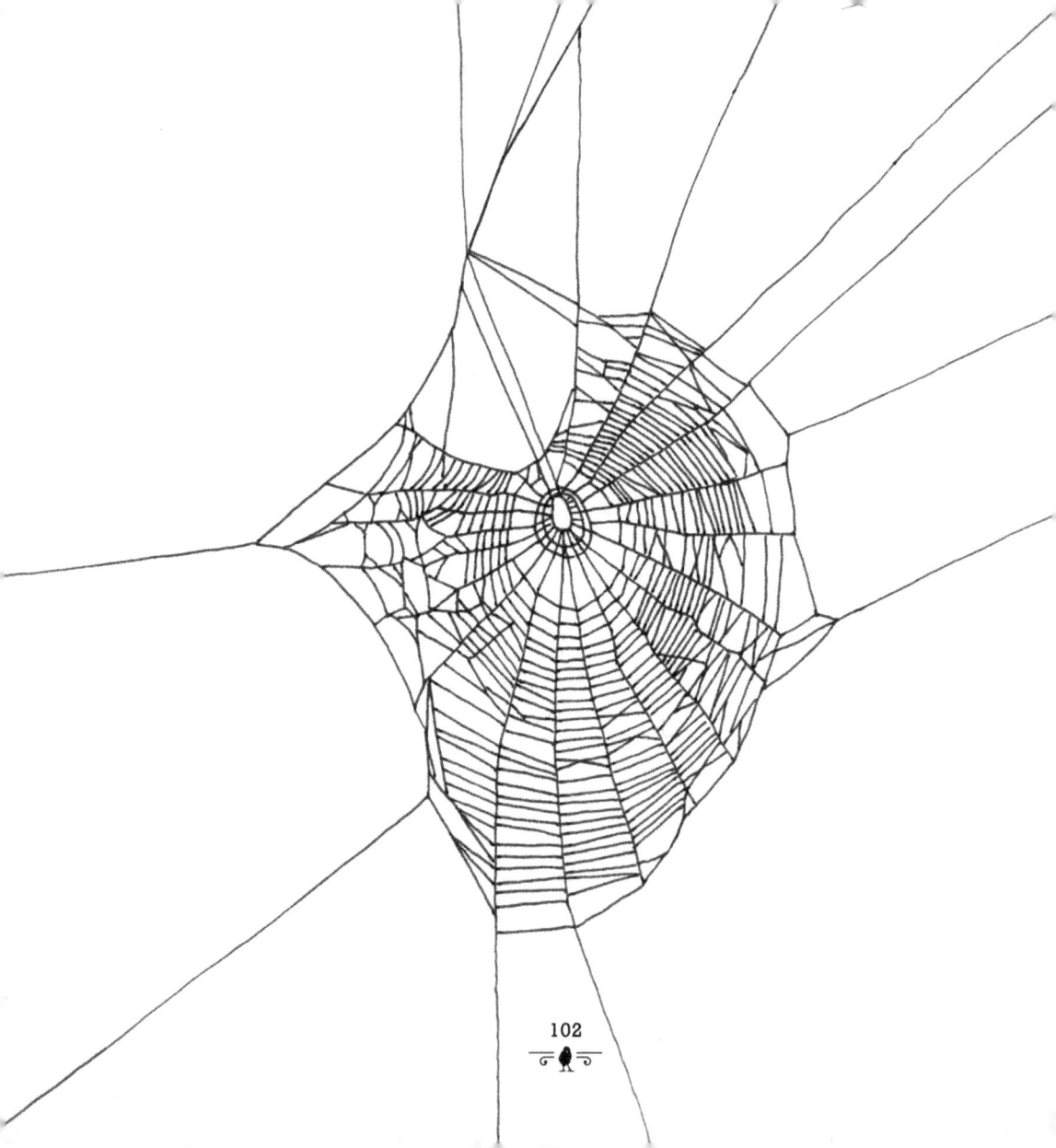

Cancer

Granddaddy died from cancer when I was little. I don't remember him. I have impressions of memories from stories and photos but nothing of him directly.

I've been told he gave me one of my first pets—a pony. I have a photo of me, in diapers and barely walking, and him with the pony. As the story goes, both the mare and the pony got into a chicken house and ate too much chicken feed. That caused them to founder and then die before anyone could help them. Grandma showed me once where they were buried. They're down in a hollow behind where the pigs used to be penned up—lots of blackberry bushes and things. Nice place. Odd, the things you remember.

I was the only grandchild he knew. And I heard stories later from his friends from when he would take me with him to go visit. We would go to the gas station—a hub of male social activity—and sit with his buddies, get a soft drink and a pack of nabs, and gossip. Don't laugh—that was a good day! These men were a little older and had mostly retired anyway. And yes, men sat around and gossiped too.

Or we'd go to another place I only remember as some type of garage. This one was where his friend always called me a little boy because I had very short hair. Apparently, as the story goes, it would make me very mad. Now that I think about it, I got picked on a lot. I was the only child and an only child with a lot of adults. Makes for an easy target!

He may have already been sick with cancer during all that time. I don't know. But somewhere in those early years, he just wasn't there anymore. I don't remember him dying or a funeral or anything. I may not have gone. But he was missing, and at some point I asked Grandma where he was.

I have the vague memory of Grandma explaining cancer to me. I don't remember the time or place, and I don't remember the exact wording, but this is the impression that was left with me.

Granddaddy was sick inside where you couldn't see it. What he had was like a spider web with a bad spider on it. The spider was making a web inside him. And as the spider made the web bigger, it was hurting him inside and making him sicker.

I don't know, or I don't remember, if she explained dying to me. But after all these years, I think it was a pretty good explanation to a very little person of a complicated issue—cancer. I still think of that bad spider any time someone talks about having cancer. And I truly appreciate she took such an effort to help me understand.

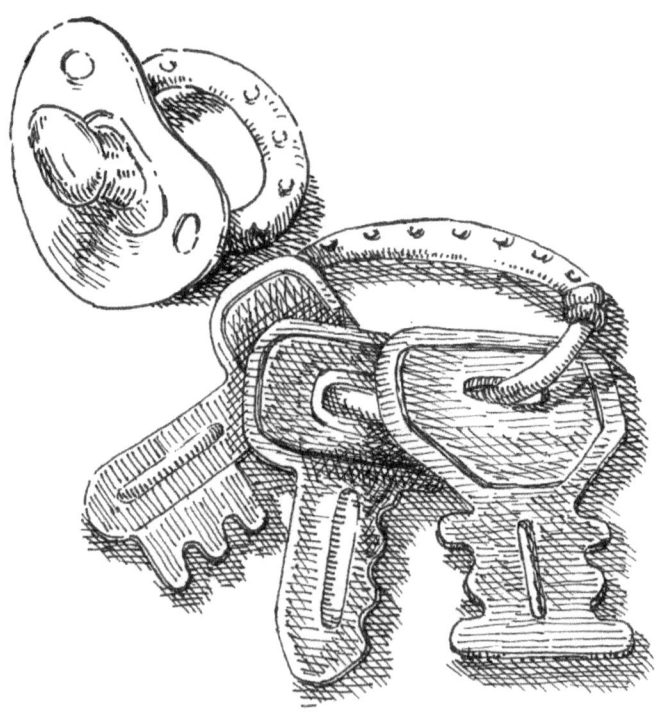

You Will Have Children

I knew when I was an early teen I did not want to have my own children. I didn't know why or have any particular reason or feelings against children. I just didn't want my own.

One summer day, out in Grandma's yard shelling peas from a morning in the garden, the subject came up. There were several of us out there. Someone—I don't remember who—said something to me about "when you have children." Not thinking quickly enough to not reply, I popped off that I wasn't going to have children. It was on from there. That was the *wrong* response!

You have to remember the timing. When I was that age, it was assumed—very strongly—that young women would go to school, get married, and start having children—in that order. Now, we have a whole generation of young women who are not planning to have them at all or who are putting off having children until later. It's "normal" now but was not then.

After my response, the next few minutes were filled with ranting lectures from a couple of the people in the yard that I "WOULD" have children, after getting married of course, and that I "WOULD" not ever say that again. I remember just staring at the people lecturing me. Grandma was not one of them. She didn't say anything at all on the subject. And I let it go telling myself to move on and not mention it again. As the lone teenager in the group, sometimes it was best to just hush up.

What you need to know here is that I never have liked—and do not to this day—being told what I'm going to do. I'd learned, mostly, to just not answer questions like that, to allow that person to assume and answer it for themselves. Made life a whole lot easier and still does. Then I just went about my business and did what I wanted anyway. But that time, I wasn't thinking.

Another day that summer, it was just Grandma and me sitting on the steps to her backdoor. "Jenny, why don't you want children?" Grandma asked. There was no tension or judgment or lecturing in the question.

"I don't know Grandma," I said. "I just don't want them."

Then she surprised me! "If you don't want to have and care for your own children, then don't have them. And don't let anyone tell you to have them.

Children are a great joy if you want them but also a great responsibility whether you want them or not. You be who you are and do what you want with your life."

I was floored! I remember just staring at her unable to comment. What she was telling me was not something I would think a grandmother would ever say. Every mother and grandmother I know are usually adamant about having children.

In typical Grandma fashion, she was telling me it's OK to not do what I was expected to do. She knew I was an independent person, good or bad. And she knew I would do what I wanted over what other people wanted, good or bad. But to hear her say it's OK to do what you want was the best thing she could have ever said. Loved this woman!

She also suggested, quite bluntly, I shouldn't push the subject with the lecturers from the pea-shelling day. "Maybe it's better we just keep this conversation and your preferences to ourselves for now. You do what you want and plan your own life." GOOD advice! Smart woman!

I carry that general thought with me still—not the choice about having children but planning my own life and doing what I want to do for me. It amazes me how many people in my world tell me what I'm going to do. I'm sure they don't realize it. But it's annoying. I've had to learn, over and over, to let it go and just hush up.

Hiding Behind the Staircase

Grandma had a philosophy: "This is my house, and I'll decide if I'm going to go to the door or if I'm going to answer the phone." I *love* this approach and still follow it to this day. You can laugh all you want to—go ahead. It works for me!

If the phone rang and she didn't feel like answering it, or was busy, she would let it ring. "I don't have time to talk to anyone right now; they'll call back if it's important." That was long before caller ID. She really had no idea who was calling and didn't care. My mother even had a set time on a set day to call if she wanted Grandma to answer the phone—Thursday evenings shortly after 7 p.m., after the long-distance rates changed for the night. Remember that?

You have to remember, back then there was usually one phone attached to the wall and it didn't have caller ID or any special rings or voice mail or anything like that. She had an old, rotary desk phone. It had about three feet of cord from the phone to the wall. And it wasn't a cord you could replace with a longer one or plug and unplug. The cord was hard wired to the phone and the wall both. Permanent!

Her phone lived in the living room on a little desk just inside that door from the kitchen. In the winter, that room was closed off to save heat. So she'd pull the phone into the kitchen and set it on a little chair just inside that door. She could close the door and still use the phone. Yep—practical, that woman!

If someone she didn't know came to the door and she didn't feel like dealing with them, she'd just ignore them and continue about her business. If they came while she was outside, I have seen her just stare at them until they felt uncomfortable enough to leave. Truly fun to watch! I hope I have the same blank stare when I do that. I try.

If someone she knew came to the door and she didn't feel like being social, that was a different story. "I don't want company, but I don't want to hurt their feelings." We would hide! Cut off anything running, such as the TV and certain lights, and hide behind the staircase in the hall. From there she could see cars pulling in and out and would see them leave. Afterward, if they mentioned it, she'd tell them she had "run to the neighbors" or was "out in the garden" to explain why her car was in the driveway or why the kitchen light was on. As far as I know, everyone bought it.

I picked up her opinions and to some degree her habits about unwanted infringement on my time and space. I just do it openly and without much care whether the person knows it, especially people I don't know. And if you have a clipboard or briefcase, don't even bother me! Just go on. I have the right not to go to the door and not answer the phone unless I choose to.

It's kinda fun. I can see people walking to my door from the recliner in my living room. I have sat right there and watched people look in the window and realize I'm sitting there—for some reason (they think), I obviously didn't hear the doorbell. Every single time, they will go press the doorbell again then knock on the door. They finally walk away, looking back toward the window, very confused. Too bad. Darn.

Note here: I usually go to the door for family, friends, and neighbors. Most people in my world who would come to my house already know to call first! I am by no means the typical Southerner. My house is not open territory for just anyone to wander in and visit when they want to.

No, I don't consider it rude. My house is just that—my house—and

I reserve the right not to deal with uninvited people if I don't want to. Period. End of discussion.

My phones are also at my discretion. Even with caller ID, there are times I just don't want to deal with the person calling. And sorry to my family and friends, even you are subject to this. Sometimes I just don't want to chat or gossip or hear any noise that will mess up my day. And you know who you are!

I usually don't answer the phone when I'm driving. Now that I need reading glasses, I can't easily see who's calling. So I'm not going to risk my life—or anyone on the road around me—to answer a call that can probably wait a few minutes. Also goes for texts, which I HATE getting to begin with. But that's a whole other topic.

I also don't answer my phone if I'm with someone, whether it's a friend at lunch or a client in a meeting. It's rude. When I leave that person, I'll check messages and call back. That's not too much to deal with.

I'll ignore the phone and email if I'm working on something and don't want the distractions. Sometimes you just need to focus on something. There's a cool little button on my phone that controls ringer volume. I know where it is, and I use it!

Some of my friends and clients have a hard time with that. One client asked me once why I didn't answer the phone when he called. "Jenny, you said to call you when I could. Why didn't you answer?" I asked him how he would feel if I was talking to or meeting with him and interrupted him to answer a call from someone else. It took him a couple minutes to figure that out. Amazing! Have we really become that rude and self-important?

So what started out as a fun game with Grandma hiding from her friends when they came to visit became a staple way of life in my house. My husband just laughs, but he doesn't go to the door or answer the phone either. He obviously—I'm assuming—agrees with me.

My house phone is the number I give to people who have some reasonable need to have it—family, medical, utilities, insurance, people like that—and the number I give when I "have to" give a phone number—pharmacy or discount card at the grocery store. That way I can screen the calls. I'd bet 90 percent of them are junk anyway: political polls, insurance sales calls, or the computer calling about a doctor's appointment. I don't need to answer those calls. And 80 percent of that 90 percent occur during the early evening when we're eating supper. I am NOT going to be on the phone while I'm trying to eat supper. No! Answering machines and voice mails are wonderful things.

My cell phones are for work and me—again, purely at my discretion and for me to decide the use of.

My work phone gets used for work stuff. During the workday. Not on weekends, holidays, or nights.

All this comes back to an original point. My house, my door, my phones. I'll answer them as I see fit. Or not! It's not a good solution for everyone. But it is for me. And it was for Grandma! *Loved* hiding behind the staircase, giggling about the secret she and I knew.

MEMORY MOMENTS

Saturday night at Grandma's was all about Lawrence Welk! That's how Grandma rolled. I remember the bubbles and the orchestra. That's about it. But she loved that show.

My Fav! Sweet Tater Pies!

OK, what is it when older people tell you they eat bacon and cook with grease and eat all the salt they want and then tell you they have very few issues with their health, but my doctors fuss at me when I tell them what I eat? What is that?!

My doctors have fits when I tell them what I eat in a normal day or what I grew up eating. But that's the stuff I grew up on. Grandma's house was filled with fried foods, lard, and bacon grease. The woman put bacon grease in boiled potatoes!

Personal side note here: bacon is probably the best food ever created with fried chicken and cheeseburgers running a tie for close second. Just so you know.

Relax. I have toned down my grease intake—a lot. And the salt. And the sugar. How boring. But I get it. My life style is not my grandmother's.

Here's my theory: Grandma (and many other older people in her same situation) was able to eat that way—and me when I was little—because they didn't add processed food into their diets. They didn't run out for fast food every day for lunch. She didn't keep junk food in the house. She was also on her feet most of the day, working. So they worked off most of what they ate with natural, built-in exercise. You could have all the biscuits and gravy you wanted because you worked it off in the fields or with the animals.

I sit for a living. I sit at a computer for hours and hours every day. I go to the gym to get exercise most mornings. I pay to sweat my food off. How funny is that?

Grandma's kitchen was a wonderful place. On a farm, you grew most of the food you ate. We had veggies from her gardens all year—fresh, canned, or frozen. We raised and killed our own meat. And the chickens and cows gave us eggs, milk, and butter. That is some GOOD eatin'!

The only things I remember Grandma buying at the grocery store were things like sugar, salt, coffee, and flour—staples. She would occasionally buy peanut butter and hotdogs for me—haha. There was a certain brand of hotdog that I loved! They were bright red. She never cooked them. I would eat one right out of the pack, carrying it in my hand. And no, my hand was probably not all that clean. A little dirt in my diet didn't hurt a thing.

Everything else came from the farm. I remember going into the smokehouse to get jars of beans and maybe a couple slices of ham off the shoulders for the next week's meals. And she always had pots of some type of beans or peas cooking. If I was around, she knew I loved Dixie Lea field peas. Then she might also have a pot of green beans cooking. Whew, good stuff.

Here's the fun part: Grandma seasoned with fatback or bacon grease. Try telling a doctor today you cook with fatback, and they'll have all kinds of fits! I made a joke once to a cardiologist that bacon grease helped grease my arteries to make the blood flow better. He almost fell off his little stool. I thought it was funny. He didn't!

So while I'm here, let me share with you some of my favorite foods from Grandma's. Her boiled taters were more like tater soup. She added bacon grease and flour to make the soup thicker. I've already talked enough about pots of beans or peas.

She made good biscuits, especially for the next day when you cut them in half, added butter, and toasted them just so the very edges were a little crunchy. I still do that now. Love to make biscuits just to have them for the next couple of days. Mine aren't as good, but they'll do. Sometimes the memory is the best part anyway.

GREAT cornbread! I have mastered cornbread, so happy to say! There isn't much better than a plate of cornbread covered in slightly salty green beans and green bean juice. Ooohhh buddy, that is some good eatin'. And her green beans did not have tomatoes in them. That's just wrong.

My fav—sweet tater pies! *That* was my absolute favorite. I've learned since, she made them different than sweet potato pies you get from the grocery store or in a restaurant. She didn't put cinnamon in them. She'd make dozens of pies for me each year in the fall when the sweet potatoes were fresh. I think I was the only one in the family who ate them. Good! More for me. It took me years to find a recipe that was close enough. But I did. And I usually have a couple in the freezer.

The one regret I have about Grandma's kitchen: when I was old enough to want to learn how to cook, she was past the point of being able to teach me. All her cooking knowledge was in her head. At some point she just couldn't get it out well enough for me to decipher. Those pinches and "some" measurements weren't clear enough to work with.

I've had to find some recipes and piece them together to get close. And of course, not adding fatback or bacon grease does make a difference. Relax, Doc, I'm not adding them.

If you'll notice, I talked about a lot of beans and peas. Many meals were just that—beans of some sort and taters. We didn't eat much meat as I remember—or maybe I didn't. I was just as happy with the peas or beans and taters. Still am.

But the meat thing does bring up another tradition at Grandma's house. Full disclosure here: if you're squeamish about farm animals and what usually happens to them, move to the next story.

As long as I can remember, the day after Thanksgiving was "hog killing day." Actually, it was a hog and a cow, at least. Granddaddy and my uncle would kill the animals and "get them ready." I have a vague memory early on of the women processing and cutting the meat at the house. Later on after Granddaddy passed, my uncle started taking the animals to the butcher. The butcher at the grocery store would cut and pack the meat for you.

Those first few years with the butcher, I remember the meat coming back in tubs, and the women would pack it into bundles. They wrapped it in white butcher paper. Later, they had the butcher prepack the meat for them.

Notice I said "the women." On Grandma's farm, and probably most others at that time, men and women had very different jobs. Men tended the grounds, fields, and large animals. The women picked and processed garden goods and meat after the animals were butchered. Not wrong or right—just was.

The animals killed that weekend fed Grandma (and Granddaddy when he was alive), my family, my uncle's family, and Ms. B and Mr. F (their kids were grown and gone by that time) all year.

Fun story here: On that day, Ms. B would start a fire and have a big black pot of boiling grease. She would cook cracklins. Think of pork rinds you get in the tater chip aisle. But Ms. B's cracklins were the real thing. When they were done, she'd lay them out on a wood railing to dry and cool. We'd eat on them all day!

Think about that for a minute. That railing was part of a fence. It was out in the weather all year, in all conditions. She would wash it down a little but didn't sterilize it or anything. Amazing isn't it!? And just for more thought, we drank right out of the well faucet and water hose too! Sorry, I find this part very funny with all the sanitizers and mess around today. Sometimes a little dirt is a good thing.

Back to the story. Ms. B would always get the heads and feet. I never saw the final product she made with them—and I didn't want to. I can imagine. Enough said on that one!

Ham shoulders were hung in the smokehouse (the storage building) in cloth bags. When you wanted ham, you cut off what you wanted and rehung the rest. For reference, this is "country ham"—the salty stuff.

The other meat was usually stored at Grandma's in a big freezer. Then when we wanted something, we just took a few packs home.

Chickens were easy. There were always chickens around. It was a chicken farm after all. Having fresh chicken for supper was easy.

I think it worked well. And we had homegrown meat to go with our homegrown veggies all year.

We even had our own milk and butter when I was little. My uncle loved milk—good thing we had a ready supply on the farm.

So back to my first point. Growing up we had what I consider "clean" and "fresh" food to eat. Adding a little grease or fatback and salt didn't do as much damage as it does now. It didn't add to the overall intake because there wasn't salt and other chemicals already added to the food before we got to it. And it was so much easier to cook all day—Grandma was home all the time. There was always something cooking.

But now, I don't always have time to cook. I try to cook on days I'm home for several hours. It does help. I do eat better when I take the time to plan and cook my meals ahead. And I do *love* having leftover peas or beans for a couple days! Nothing like a big bowl of beans and corn bread. I'm telling ya.

CHRISTMAS NOTE FROM GRANDMA

You are growing up to be a real nice little girl, and we love you with all our hearts. I'm afraid another grandchild will never mean to us what you have. Always try to live like God wants you to live, and you won't have any trouble solving the many problems you will face later on.

Always ask his guidance in anything, and he will help. All we have to do is ask him because he loves every one of us. You will have problems, but they are so much easier with his help. Without his help, we can't solve anything. We have to have his help to be strong people.

We love you.

Kitty

I was older, near the end or just after college I think. A little cat showed up at Grandma's. At that point, she didn't have any pets, and I think she was lonely.

She kept the cat and named her Kitty. Not very original, but it worked. She was small with short, grey hair. Sweet cat! She followed Grandma everywhere and seemed to have the perfect temperament for an older person: she was already litter-box trained, and she didn't cry a lot or get on furniture or even scratch things. She liked to go outside and wander around during the day but would come running when Grandma called her.

On one visit, Grandma told me she thought Kitty was "sent" to keep her company. That struck me hard. That was the first time I'd heard her express anything about being lonely or alone. I realized Grandma was lonely—hit me like a brick right in the face. She'd lost her driver's license, as had most of her friends. And she couldn't get out and go and do like she used to.

I think she really thought "someone" had sent this little cat to keep her company. And by "someone" I think she thought Granddaddy. Every time I went to visit, I was so happy to see Kitty!

It wasn't too many years later that Grandma passed. My uncle, who lived next door, was taking care of Kitty until it was decided who would take her. Kitty would wander around the house crying, looking for Grandma.

A few days after the funeral, Kitty was gone. We never saw her again. Kinda makes you wonder, *was* Kitty sent to keep Grandma company? I choose to believe she was. And I'm grateful for Kitty's companionship.

MEMORY MOMENTS

There were gourds everywhere at Grandma's. She had several she used for drinking water out in the gardens or at the chicken houses and barns. There was even one hanging out on the pumphouse by the spigot. They were great! Cut a hole in the ball and clean it out to get a perfectly good water cup.

You Don't Need My Phone Number

One of Grandma's "things" was secrecy, or privacy might be a better word. She hated answering questions from people who didn't "need" to know the answers. During my teenage and college years, I really began to understand. This is now a core belief for me. I apply it across the board!

Every once in a while someone would come to the house looking for something or someone, or trying to sell something. If Grandma went to the door or got caught out in the yard, she was very vague, short, and to the point. It didn't help that she hated uninvited company.

Here is one example I was privileged to witness. This was a thing of beauty!

Man drove up while we were out in the yard messing with some flowers and plants.

"Ma'am," he said, "I'm looking for Mr. ___. Does he live here?"

It happened to be my grandfather he was looking for. He had passed away several years earlier.

Grandma, who did turn around and face the man: "No." Short and sweet but not ugly.

"But I have this address listed for him." And he proceeded to try and show her his paperwork on his little clipboard.

Grandma: silence. She just looked at him. After all this time, I get it. He wasn't asking a question, he was making a statement. So she felt no need to give a response either way. LOVE doing that to people.

Man, finally after several seconds: "Can you tell me where he lives?"

Grandma: "No." Again, not ugly, just a matter of fact.

The guy finally got frustrated and left. It was so funny to me. Grandma was deadpan the whole time and didn't even flinch when he left. She wasn't rude or ugly to him; she obviously just didn't feel the need to engage. We went back to what we were doing with her plants without missing a beat.

I apply this same philosophy still today. Not everyone needs to know whatever it is they are asking about. And honestly, just 'cause you have a clipboard and some information does not mean I feel the need to verify or add to that information. So there!

Most of what I run into these days centers around people asking for personal information they don't need but are told to collect.

I went into a store several years ago to buy a baby gift from a baby registry list. There is very little chance I'll ever go back in that particular store again—not many babies in my world. And I was paying with cash—ultimate anonymity! The cashier asked me for my phone number. "Why do you need that?" She gave me the standard answer about the register screen going through questions she was supposed to ask.

"No, you don't need my phone number." She froze with a very confused look on her face. She didn't know what to do. Apparently no one had ever refused to give her a phone number. Then she told me it was required, and she couldn't scan my item until I gave her my phone number and she could get past that screen.

It really wasn't worth my time, on that day, to argue the point. "OK, 123-456-7899 is my phone number." Teenage cashier—I got the look! You know the eyes rolling, OMG look? I've given it, so I recognize it well. But I stayed the course, not flinching or offering any further comment. She finally—finally—gave in and entered the number I gave her.

Now, looking back, it was hysterical. When that happens to me now, I have *way* more fun with it. At the time it really bugged me. Why does that store, that I'll probably never go back into, need to know my phone number if I don't want to give it to them? Things have changed a little. I've had that same thing happen since, and the cashier was able to skip the question. Some progress at least. Even though now they ask for an email address. NO!

Another one that really gets on my last nerve and usually sets a negative tone for the whole conversation: when you call me, the first thing out of your mouth should NOT be "Is ___ there?" You do not need to know that until I know who you are and what you want. You called me! You interrupted my day and my time. I do not feel the need to explain to an unknown caller who is and is not present in my house at any given time. A little common sense would be to tell me who you are *before* you start demanding to know who's at home.

I have the same general opinion about calls to my business phone as well. And I expect someone calling my business to have a little better procedure. When you call me—or anyone else—

remember, I don't read minds and may not just know who you are or what you want. Help me out here—introductions please.

But wait! There's yet more to my "no need to know" rule.

Now having adopting this "no need to know" attitude, here comes the really fun part. When I feel like messing with someone or when I'm in the mood to play, I'll answer the "exact" question asked with "exact" answers instead of the drawn-out explanations they are expecting. That's what Grandma did in the example above. "No" was the best and only answer needed to the question. It drives people nuts. "Jenny, that's a beautiful sweater. Is it new?" "Thank you. No."

I know—it's a little cruel. Too bad. Grandma started it. I'm just carrying it forward—and enjoying every bit of it! The hard part is keeping a straight face.

Masking Tape

One of my favorite Christmas stories, with one Christmas present in particular: one year, I gave Grandma a Living Bible with large print for Christmas. You've seen them—dark green with a soft padded cover. They were very popular for several years—and may still be?

We put up her Christmas tree and left her presents there, with the ones she had for us, to make the tree look "full." That was the weekend after Thanksgiving.

I was still too young to really go buy my own presents for anyone. So my mother bought them, and I gave them. Good system! But by doing that, she knew what my gift to Grandma was. And I don't know if she told Grandma what it was or if Grandma just got nosy. Maybe both.

We went to visit every Saturday. The next week I noticed the wrapping looked different. And I noticed it had been rewrapped—with masking tape. Really? I didn't say anything. I just laughed—to myself—and assumed Grandma got nosy and wanted to see what it was. OK with me. I guess sometimes you just need a sneak peak.

What I didn't know or realize—she had been taking it to church on Sundays and using it. She was already writing it in during Sunday school lessons.

Christmas Day, we arrived for our normal happenings at Grandma's house—lunch, presents, and fun. She opened the present and made a "big deal" about it. "Whoo hoo! Just what I wanted!" I couldn't help it. "Grandma, you already knew what it was. You've opened it and rewrapped it."

"No, I haven't."

"Grandma, you used masking tape." Busted!

It was SO funny! "Well, Jenny, I just wanted to start using it. The large print is easier to read."

We *all* just hee-hawed! How do you get mad at that? It turned into a Christmas tradition—checking all the presents each week to see if she had opened them. I didn't really mind. I just enjoyed picking at her about it.

She used that bible for years. There are notes from sermons and Sunday school lessons all through it. When she passed, that was one of the bibles I brought home. Just seeing it brings such good memories.

CHRISTMAS NOTE FROM GRANDMA

Christmas is a time for showing our love to one another. It all began because God wanted to show love to his people, by giving them his son to die on the cross to save us from our sins. Jesus is love in action. When Jesus was born the wise men took him presents. So I think we are supposed to remember the ones we love on this day. The wise men did not take expensive presents, so I don't think we should overdo it. But we can express our love in a simple way.

A Christian has four anchors in life to live by that non-Christians do not have. Because we are Christians doesn't mean we do not sin (we are all human). But it does mean that we don't practice sin, and when we do sin we ask forgiveness.

1) The anchor of Hope helps us weather the storms of life.
2) The anchor of Duty (love) keeps us stable and well balanced, no matter how rough the going gets.
3) The anchor of Prayer is for the soul. When we stop praying we cast away an anchor.
4) Faith anchor—the cross of our Lord Jesus Christ—the knowledge that Christ died for us.

Frustrated people have no anchors. For praise—walk with the knowledge that we are never alone.

For beautiful eyes always see the good.

MEMORY MOMENTS

There are some things only a grandma would allow. A lot of mornings my breakfast was cereal—corn flakes. At Grandma's I was allowed to add all the sugar I wanted to my cereal. How cool is that!

Adult Female

I was in college, had a part time job, and was getting ready to graduate and trying to find a real job. One day while visiting Grandma, sitting in the yard, I was telling her about some stuff happening around me—the "noise" in my world.

She started laughing.

"Grandma, what's so funny?"

"Jenny, I think you'll reach 'Adult Female' so much sooner than most women."

"What?"

Hang on here—if you haven't reached "Adult Female," it might be a little confusing. If you have, you'll understand every word!

Grandma's theory—and I've seen it over and over so many times since she explained it to me—was that most women reach a point in their lives when they become self-aware and self-empowered. She called it "Adult Female."

It's that point when you, as an adult and as a female, decide that you no longer really care about what other people think of you. YOU are the only person you have to answer to or impress.

Below are some of the characteristics, explanations, and examples Grandma used to help me understand.

Adult Females wear clothes they want to wear because they feel good and look good in them, not because that's what the fashion magazines or their friends say it's what they should be wearing. Don't misunderstand—Grandma wasn't talking about wearing your PJs to the grocery store. She meant wearing clothes that fit, clothes that look good on your body shape and size, and then being comfortable in them. You can tell just by watching a woman if she's comfortable in her clothes.

There is a point, regardless of your weight, shape, or height, when you decide to wear clothes designed for you specifically. We all do it. Think about the last time you looked at those jeans from high school—trust me, you will not ever be able to fit in those things again.

Even if you're the same weight, your shape has changed over the years. Let it go, baby. Let it go. That's not a bad thing. Rhinestone-covered, low-riding bell-bottoms at your age—NO.

Adult Females have and voice their opinions, even if they aren't politically correct or don't fit with other people around them. You are allowed to like or dislike anyone or anything you want. It's OK to like a different political candidate than your friend or family member. It's OK to like a different football team than the people you work with. It's OK to dislike a particular color even though your teenage daughter just has to have her room painted that color.

Opinions—differing opinions—are among the things that make us strong. Follow your team and your favorite candidate without being apologetic to other people. Just be careful—opinions are volatile things. We Adult Females are careful not to allow our opinions to become judgments of other people.

This one gets me into trouble. So I've learned to have opinions but not voice them so much. The arguments that ensue just aren't worth the trouble for me. I love the people I've allowed into my inner circle, even when we don't always have the same opinions. And I don't care about anyone else's opinions. So maybe sometimes, just hushing up is the best choice for me. It's much easier.

But understand—if you ask for my opinion and if I choose to tell you my opinion, don't fuss if it's not what you want to hear. I will shut you down. I am not going to argue with anyone over my opinions. I believe everyone's opinions are correct to them. Opinions are based on information, history, experience, and "feelings." My opinions are mine to have and hold as I see fit. So there!

Adult Females are self-confident and aware of their strengths and weaknesses. This is a biggie! Most women are raised or taught to wallow in their faults, to be "sorry" for everything. NO! Come on, ladies—let us move on from this! We all have strengths—figure out what yours are and use them to your advantage. We all have weaknesses—figure out what yours are and take the steps needed to lessen their impact on you. Notice I did not say "overcome them."

One of Grandma's things was to know your weaknesses and just let them alone. One example she gave me was a fear of something. If you have a fear of snakes, that might be considered a weakness. But do you really need to overcome that fear of snakes? Or do you just need to be aware of it and take steps necessary to not be around snakes? Will overcoming your fear of snakes help you?

If you live on a farm, overcoming a fear of snakes might be necessary. If your world is mostly in a downtown region of the city filled with high-rise buildings and concrete, you probably won't encounter many snakes. So sometimes, just letting that "weakness" sit over there out of the way works better than expending energy on it.

Adult Females own things because they fit their needs and lifestyles, not because someone else has them. One good example of this one is phones. There are several Adult Females in my world who don't have, nor do they want, a smart phone. They have flip phones and are perfectly happy with them. It's all they need and all they want.

Other examples are your car and your house. I live in what most people around me consider a small house. It's big enough for my family and me. I don't need 4,000 square feet of space to fill with junk or clean. I also don't need a brand new car every two to three years. I have a car that suits what and who I need to carry and where I need to go. I, personally, don't need a $60,000 luxury car I have to worry about every time I leave it in a parking lot.

Adult Females are loving, supportive, and compassionate with everyone around them. You share more of yourself than you realize. Other than "personal time," such as exercise and meditation, your partners, spouses, family members, and close friends always come first. They feel your love and support, even if they don't realize it. When they thrive and succeed, you do as well.

I know—that may sound backward. But it's not. Grandma was adamant about supporting loved ones and making sure they succeeded and flourished. Remember before her telling me I didn't have to have children if I didn't want to? I see that as the ultimate Adult Female response now that I understand it. She was telling me to do what was right for me. She knew it would be the best thing for me and would make me better able to succeed in what I wanted to do.

Those are simple examples, but you get my point, yes?

Now having said all that, I want to make the main point. Adult Females have families, husbands, and friends who "get it." The families don't consider this female relative the "bossy one." Husbands aren't intimidated or put off. Friends enjoy the good moods and positive attitude when around them. All these people understand that they have strong women at their sides, at their backs, and leading the way.

These women have an inner strength! They're naturally not bitchy or bossy or obnoxious. They are just strong and aware and confident. And they know it! They don't have to boss people around or be the "bitch" in the office. They know how to work with their coworkers. They know how to help the entire team succeed. They take pleasure and pride in other people's accomplishments and successes.

I had a peer once tell me something that has stuck with me. Now I think it fits perfectly here. She told me she loved to see her staff being promoted out of her department or even to other companies. Her manager hated it. He hated having to spend money hiring and training people and wanted them all to stay "in their place."

She explained it to me. She considered it a compliment. That employee learned enough either about that job or with their skill sets to be valuable in better positions. She saw it as helping that employee learn, grow, and move on to bigger, better things in life. That promotion might have a raise the employee's family needs. Or it might take them to a city they've always wanted to live in. How can an Adult Female be upset when someone in her sphere of influence betters themselves?

I understood that later. When I had my first staff member get promoted to another department, I understood. She would get a huge raise and be allowed more opportunities for advancement beyond that position. That explanation reset my entire thinking on training people. That day I intentionally started training staff. Anything they wanted to learn (pertaining to their jobs or advancement) was fair game.

You know the funny part? It made my job easier! The culture in that company had too much secrecy, too many people who knew their one thing and wouldn't allow anyone else to learn it. You know what happens—that one person is out sick, and the whole system grinds to a halt.

I managed an IT department. All of the sudden I was not the only person who could do things. I started showing staff how to handle simple server problems and debug some normal computer issues. It was *freeing*! One place I love the word "free." And it made them much more valuable. We all won!

But back to Grandma's original point. Honestly, I think I was almost there before I even learned to talk. "Independent" little person! I've always had a mind of my own with my own opinions, likes, and dislikes. And I like it that way.

But it was fun thinking about it and listening to Grandma's explanations. At that time, I thought she'd spent her entire life on a farm in the small town she lived in. What would this woman know about "women" and their struggles to be themselves?

Funny aside here: it wasn't until I moved to Charlotte after college that I learned Grandma was born and raised in Charlotte. Really? How come that never came up? She and her sister, as young women, had an apartment, had jobs, and went to college in downtown Charlotte. I was amazed!

These women—Adult Females—can juggle home, family, career, and anything else that comes up, but still miss things occasionally and still make mistakes. Then they accept, learn, and move on to the next thing. They have a positive outlook on life, mainly because they control their own paths. They're genuinely happy and care about everyone around them.

I think my favorite part of Grandma's whole theory is the right to make mistakes and move on. Remember earlier in the book, I talked about Grandma's ability to make things "OK." It's OK. That fits here. She was teaching me this theory the whole time.

Adult Females do miss things; they do make mistakes; they're wrong on occasion. But the world doesn't stop because of that. They acknowledge, they learn, they fix if necessary, and they move on. They don't get so caught up in blame or guilt or any other negatives that will hold them back. It's OK. Works for me! I'm "adult" enough to handle it.

To this day, I love meeting women who are comfortable in their own skin, have confidence in themselves, and live their lives to their own satisfaction. How can you not admire a woman who knows who she is and *loves* herself for it?

One final thought on this whole Adult Female theory. Grandma waited till the end of our conversation to share this little tidbit.

Once I began to understand, she told me her other title for it—"Inner Bitch." I like that one! Much More Better! I've always loved the titles "Bitch," "Broad," and "Dame." Somehow those words remind me of strong women with stronger attitudes.

Part of Grandma's whole theory was when a woman reaches Adult Female, her inner voice—or Inner Bitch—is finally able to communicate with her and help her navigate her world. *That* is what helps that woman step from just being an adult female to Adult Female.

All women have an inner voice—intuition, instinct, whatever you call yours. Most of us, especially in the South, are raised to ignore and control our inner voices, so we appear more "lady like" and "demure." Bull! That mess needs to stop!

My Inner Bitch and I have become hard and fast friends. She is my strength and allows me to be my own person, control my own environment, say yes or no as needed, and move easily through all the "noise" around me. She allows me to be the best me I can be at that moment.

That's what my Inner Bitch allows me to do—take control for my betterment.

Funny story here: I was dating a guy during college. He got it. He understood! One weekend he went to the beach with his buddies. He came back with a present for me. Cool! It was a gold necklace—a thin chain with a charm on it. The charm was one word repeated three times, stacked atop each other: Bitch, Bitch, Bitch. I LOVED it! And that was before Grandma clued me in.

Grandma used to tell me when I was little I was an "independent" child. Some other people in my world called it "stubborn" or "bull headed." I didn't understand at the time, obviously. Then this revelation of her theory about an Adult Female mindset really kicked in. Though I'm not sure I fully understood or felt I had reached that level at the time of our conversation. But I wanted to get there as soon as possible!

Now, I know exactly what she means. I *feel* it! And I *like* it! And I think it makes me a better person, a better woman.

I Wonder

I hope you enjoyed my stories about Grandma and the lessons she left me with. I thought, and still think, she was a very smart woman!

I mentioned at one point, I had grown up thinking she had lived on a farm all her life, that somehow her world had been narrow and sheltered. Not so. When I moved to Charlotte, I learned she was born in Charlotte. At one point, she and her sister lived in an apartment downtown, had jobs, and attended college. I was floored!

I wonder, sometimes, what she would have become had she stayed the course she was on. I wonder, sometimes, what would have happened if her Adult Female had been allowed to live, learn, and grow somewhere other than that peaceful little farm I remember.

Oh well, things worked out the way they should have. And I had the best Grandma EVER!

About the Author

Jenny Prevatte is the daughter of farmers and mechanics from "small town" North Carolina. Though she has a Bachelor of Science in mechanical engineering from North Carolina State University, her career path took her into computers, graphic design, web design, and finally online marketing.

She started her own business on the side in 1991 while working for a regional food broker and then for a national trade association. She was primarily the "computer nerd" for the office. As time went on, she learned more about graphic design and then about web design as the Internet came into play. What she did for those companies as an employee, she also did through her side business for friends and clients.

All along, her time spent with Grandma, as an "independent little person," was working its way to the surface. She eventually realized that she wasn't a good employee. She didn't play the game well. She needed the freedom to do her own thing and not be tied to someone else's clock and agenda.

When her position was eliminated in 2005, she took her side business full time. That's when Grandma's lessons came to life. She could apply many of Grandma's personal lessons to interactions with her friends, clients, and associates.

She has continued to build her business and loves telling people she comes from farmers and mechanics. It fits with her personality and the way she does business. Grandma made sure Jenny was well grounded with a healthy respect for other people.

The author and her Grandma circa 1968.

Available at WhenGrandmaTeachesYouToLie.com

www.ingramcontent.com/pod-product-compliance
Lightning Source LLC
Chambersburg PA
CBHW081340080526
44588CB00017B/2698